The ULTiMATe BOOK of PRETEEN GAMES

Revised and Updated

Group's R.E.A.L. Guarantee® to you:

This Group resource incorporates our R.E.A.L. approach to ministry—one that encourages long-term retention and life transformation. It's ministry that's:

Relational
Because learner-to-learner interaction enhances learning and builds Christian friendships.

Experiential
Because what learners experience through discussion and action sticks with them up to 9 times longer than what they simply hear or read.

Applicable
Because the aim of Christian education is to equip learners to be both hearers and doers of God's Word.

Learner-based
Because learners understand and retain more when the learning process takes into consideration how they learn best.

The Ultimate Book of Preteen Games (Revised and Updated)
Copyright © 2001 Group Publishing, Inc.

Visit our Website: **group.com**

Credits

Contributing Authors: Tom Aron, Ivy Beckwith, Laurie Casteñeda, Holly Henderson, Michele Howe, Cortland Kirkeby, Jim Kochenburger, Julie Meiklejohn, Heather Parrott, Christina Schofield, Helen Turnbull, and Paul Woods
Editor: Jim Hawley
Senior Editor: Karl Leuthauser
Chief Creative Officer: Joani Schultz
Copy Editor: Dena Twinem

Art Director: Jean Bruns
Designer: iDesignEtc.
Print Production Artist: Tracy K. Donaldson
Illustrator: Harry Pulver Jr.
Cover Art Director: Jeff A. Storm
Cover Designer: Alan Furst Inc.
Cover Illustrator: Harry Pulver Jr.
Production Manager: Peggy Naylor

Unless otherwise noted, Scripture taken from the HOLY BIBLE, NEW INTERNATIONAL VERSION®. Copyright © 1973, 1978, 1984 by International Bible Society. Used by permission of Zondervan Publishing House. All rights reserved.

Library of Congress Cataloging-in-Publication Data

The ultimate book of preteen games / [contributing authors, Tom Aron ... et al.].
    p. cm.
  Includes index.
  ISBN 978-0-7644-2291-1 (alk. paper)
    1. Christian education of preteens. 2. Games in Christian education. I. Aron, Tom. II.
Group Publishing.

BV1475.9 .U46 2001
268'.432--dc21

                                                            00-052807
17 16 15 14 13 12   14 13 12 11 10 09
Printed in the United States of America.

CONTENTS
contents

Section 5: Games for Big Bunches of Preteens

Section 6: Quiet Games

Section 7: Wild & Wacky Games

Section 8: Games for Special Days

Section 9: On-the-Road Games

"**L**et's play a game!" Preteens *love* to hear these words. But what games will you play? Preteens aren't children—so they may not like to play children's games. And they may want to play some games from a youth games book, but the point might go over their heads. What to do?

You're holding the answer in your hands—*The Ultimate Book of Preteen Games!* Games designed just for preteens. More sophisticated than children's games, but not as complex as many youth games—the perfect answer!

The Ultimate Book of Preteen Games has nine types of games:

Clumpbreakers: Easy-to-prepare and quick crowdbreakers for any size group.

Clumpbuilders: Fun games to help preteens get to know each other better.

Bible-in-Me Games: Engage preteens in familiar Bible stories using these fun and creative games.

Games for Little Clusters of Preteens: A variety of games perfect for groups of ten or less.

Games for Big Bunches of Preteens: Use these games with groups of twenty or more.

Quiet Games: Challenge preteens' thinking and creative abilities with these games.

Wild & Wacky Games: Looking for *really* wild games? Look no further!

Games for Special Days: Fun games for holidays and other special days.

On-the-Road Games: Pile your preteens into a van or bus and head down the road playing these travel games.

Most games have Topic Connections that will help you pick the right game for any occasion. See the Topic Connections Index on p. 111. Look for the Game Guy Tips throughout these games to help you become The Preteen Gamemeister!

COMPETITION AND YOUR KIDS

Your kids compete for grades, friends, a spot on the baseball team—they're *always* competing. In their world there's often one winner—and lots of losers.

That's *not* how you want children to experience your class or Sunday school: as a place where there's one winner—and lots of losers. In Christ, we're *all* winners.

These games encourage cooperation, not competition. There aren't losers because everyone contributes to the group's success. Kids cheer each other on. They feel good about participating. They play for fun, not bragging rights.

But competition may still creep into the mix. Kids are conditioned to think a game needs a winner and loser, or it's not really a game at all.

Here are three competition-busting strategies to use when needed:

1. **Keep stakes low.** Don't award prizes, even if the prize is to keep playing while others have to sit down.

2. **Mix up teams part way through the game.** Whether the score is lopsided or close, arbitrarily have everyone with a birthday in a month that begins with J switch sides part way through the game. Or everyone who has shoelaces, blonde hair, or a name with more than two vowels. By the end of the game, most kids will have contributed to the "winning team."

3. **Flip a coin and award one team ten million points at the end of the third quarter.** If the score suddenly becomes 10,000,006 to 7, winning no longer matters.

CLUMPBREAKERS

For some reason preteens come in clumps. Each clump has its own identity. It may be the snotty-girl clump, the computer-geek clump, or the skater clump. The problem is that when preteens are clumped, they often act like clods. Use these games to break apart the clumps to find soil that is ready for planting. Have fun!

GET CONNECTED
getconnected

Topic Connections: You can use this game to teach about cliques, change, gangs, and fitting in.

Game Overview: Participants will form groups based on the numbers the leader calls out.

Energy Level: High

Supplies: None

Preparation: Clear away tables and chairs if necessary.

Say: **When I call out a number, you will need to form groups of that size by connecting arms with others around you. For example, if I call out "five," you'll need to hook arms with four other people for a total**

of five people. If I call out "three," you'll need to connect with two other people to form a group of three. Make sure your group isn't too big or too small.

Call out various numbers and keep the game moving quickly. Make sure you include numbers that make it impossible for everyone to find a place to fit. ◼

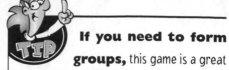

If you need to form groups, this game is a great way to do it. Just end by calling out the number equal to the size of the groups you're looking for.

POLAR MOLAR
polar molar

Topic Connections: You can use this game to teach about love by talking about how the cold gum is like a loveless heart. You can also talk about stubbornness by relating the cold gum to inflexibility.

Game Overview: Participants will race to soften frozen gum and blow a bubble.

Energy Level: Low

Supplies: Bubble gum

Preparation: Freeze packages of bubble gum twenty-four hours prior to the game.

For a genuine clumpbreaker, have a bubble-blowing contest with frozen gum. Freeze several packages of bubble gum prior to your meeting. Distribute the frozen gum to participants and watch as they race to blow the first bubble.

This game will put participants at ease and won't make anyone new feel uncomfortable. ◼

HUMAN SCRABBLE
h u m a n s c r a b b l e

Topic Connections: You can use this game to teach about fitting in, working together, and unity. You can also use it to teach preteens about gaining understanding by focusing on making meaning out of the mixed-up letters. It's a great game to teach students new words like "billet-doux."

Game Overview: Participants will join others in the group to form words out of letters worn on players' shirts.

Energy Level: Medium

Supplies: Paper, markers, stopwatch, tape

Preparation: None

To begin, distribute paper and markers and ask participants to choose a letter of the alphabet and write it on a piece of paper. When they have finished, ask them to tape the letter to their shirts.

If you go into a game thinking it won't work, you will almost certainly be proved right. However, if you make adjustments to make the game work for your group, or try something new with enthusiasm, you're almost certain to be pleasantly surprised.

Say: **You will have thirty seconds to join other players in forming words out of the letters you're wearing. Words must contain three letters or more.**

If someone picks Q have the student put a U on the paper so he or she can stay involved in the game.

Continue as long as preteens are interested. Players should form new words each round. The game could be played like musical chairs, eliminating players who don't fit into a word. ■

TRADE-OFF
t r a d e - o f f

Topic Connections: You can use this game to teach about sharing, cooperation, unity, giving, and selfishness.

Game Overview: Kids will trade multicolored candies as they learn simple facts about each other.

Energy Level: Medium

Supplies: Colored candies, resealable plastic bags

Preparation: For each student, fill a bag with three or four different-colored candies.

As kids arrive, give each person a bag of candy. Ask kids not to open the bags yet.

Tell kids that they'll use the candy to help them get to know each other. Explain that the object of the game is to trade pieces of candy with other people until each person has candies of only one color (other than the colors they started with) in their bags. Explain that this game has only three rules:

> **TIP** **You might want to** have preteens wash their hands or use individually wrapped candies. Otherwise, they may be passing more than candy.

• A person may not exchange more than one candy piece at a time.

• A person may not exchange candy pieces with the same person more than once.

• Each time a candy exchange occurs, each exchanger needs to tell the other an interesting fact about him- or herself.

When kids understand the rules, have them start mingling and exchanging candy.

After a few students have just one color of candy, have everyone share the facts they learned about each other. They can eat their candy while they share! ◼

DRUTHERS
d r u t h e r s

Topic Connections: You can use this game to teach preteens about making choices.

Game Overview: Kids will get to know each other as they express their preferences.

Energy Level: Low

Supplies: "Which Would You Choose?" handout on page 12

Preparation: none

Have kids form pairs, and explain that they're going to get to know each other better by expressing their preferences.

Tell pairs that you'll read two choices, and they'll need to tell their partners which they would choose. Explain that they shouldn't take time to think about their answers; they should just give the answer that sounds best at the time.

Read two of the "druthers" aloud, one at a time. Give partners time to explain their answers to each other. After a few rounds, have volunteers share what they learned about their partners.

Have preteens find new partners and repeat the process. ◧

TIP

If kids are interested, let them continue this game by having them come up with their own druthers for each other. You may want to make sure their choices are appropriate.

IN KNOTS
i n k n o t s

Topic Connections: You can use this game to teach about working together, or how the tangled knot is similar to working through a tangled conflict.

Game Overview: Kids will try to untangle a human knot.

Energy Level: Medium

WHICH WOULD YOU CHOOSE?

Would you rather eat...
>**vanilla ice cream** or **chocolate ice cream?**

Would you rather live...
>**on the beach** or **in the mountains?**

On vacation, would you rather go...
>**to Disneyland** or **to Alaska?**

Would you rather be...
>**an eagle** or **a horse?**

Would you rather lose your...
>**sense of sight** or **your hearing?**

Would you rather be...
>**a movie star** or **a professional athlete?**

Would you rather eat at...
>**McDonald's** or **a fancy restaurant?**

Would you rather be...
>**extremely intelligent** or **incredibly good-looking?**

Would you rather...
>**explore another planet** or **explore someone else's thoughts?**

Would you rather own...
>**your dream house** or **your dream car?**

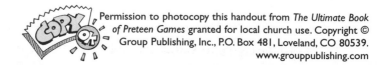

Supplies: none

Preparation: none

Have kids make a tight circle and stick their arms out toward the center. Have each person grab a hand with each of his or her hands.

Say: **It appears that we have quite a knot here. Let's work together to untie it. But whatever you do, do not let go of the hands you're holding onto right now.**

Have kids go under each other's arms to work out the human knot. You may need to help direct the process.■

WHO AM I?

w h o   a m   i ?

Topic Connections: You can use this game to teach kids about being real or being content with who God made them.

Game Overview: Kids will mingle and try to guess each other's identities.

Energy Level: Medium

Supplies: Index cards, marker, tape

Preparation: Separate index cards into pairs and then write the names of a famous couple on each pair of cards. For example, one card in a pair might say "Batman" while the other says "Robin." Write the names of couples that your kids will be familiar with. You'll need one index card for each person.

Have kids sit in a circle. Tape an index card on each person's back. Ask kids not to tell each other what's written on the index cards.

Explain that each person will need to discover the identity that's on his or her back. Kids will do this by mingling and asking each other questions about their identities. Here are the rules:

This is a great game to use if you need to form pairs!

• A person may not talk to any single person more than once.
• A person may only ask another person three questions.

• **All questions must be "yes" or "no" questions.**

Encourage kids to mingle. Explain that when a person has guessed his or her identity, he or she should put the index card on his or her front. Then the person may continue to mingle to help others discover their identities. Kids also need to figure out who their matching partners are. ◼

LINE 'EM UP
line 'em up

Topic Connections: You can use this game to teach preteens about communication.

Game Overview: Kids will get to know each other better as they line up according to categories.

Energy Level: Medium

Supplies: None

Preparation: None

Have kids stand in a circle, and explain that in a moment, you'd like them to change the order they're in by lining up according to the first letter of their first names. Tell kids where the circle "begins." So, for example, those with first names beginning with A, B, or C would be standing at one end of the circle, and those with first names beginning with letters later in the alphabet would be standing at the other end of the

> **You can play this game** using birthdays, height, or even amount of earwax build-up. Communicating some items will be more difficult without talking, such as birthdays.

circle. Tell kids that there's only one catch—they can't talk at all. Designate the point in the circle where the alphabet should start and then say "Go!"

Give kids a minute to line themselves up, and then have them go around the circle and introduce themselves. ◼

THE CANDY BAR HUNT

the candy bar hunt

Topic Connections: You can use this game to teach kids about loyalty or cliques.

Game Overview: Kids will find a partner or a team by matching parts of a candy bar and will then create a cheer about why their candy bar is the best.

Energy Level: Low to medium

Supplies: Resealable snack bags, candy bars, kitchen knife, cardboard box, tape, paper

Preparation: Gather two of each of a variety of candy bars. Cut different kinds of candy bars in half so that you have four like-pieces of candy. Place each piece in a separate snack bag. Put all the bags of candy bar pieces in a box that does not allow the kids to see what bag they are selecting when the game begins. Tape each candy bar wrapper to a sheet of paper to make a sign, and place the signs around the room.

Pass around the box and let kids draw out a snack bag. Tell kids to find a matching piece of the candy bar. Once a match is found, they should go to the sign for their candy bar and as a team make up a cheer about why their candy bar is the best. For example, a group may say, "M&M's keep us alive. But we miss red dye number 5" or "Snickers. Snickers. They're so filling. We keep eating and the dentist keeps drilling." After five minutes, call on each candy bar team to give their individual names and their cheers. After all the cheers are done, let the kids eat their candy bars.

TIP **If your group is large,** cut the candy bars in fourths, and put each piece in its own snack bag.

TIP **Keep enthusiasm high** by leading applause after each cheer is given.

CLUMP BUILDERS

Sometimes you need to break the preteen clumps apart. Sometimes you need to bring them together. You know it's time to bring them together if the discussion stays on the surface or if you have too many kids hanging out on the fringes.

EVERY BODY NEEDS SOME BODY SOMETIME

every body needs some body sometime

Topic Connections: You can use this game to teach preteens about the body of Christ or their unique gifts and talents.

Game Overview: Kids will find creative ways to form groups based on the index cards they have.

Energy Level: Medium

Supplies: Index cards, paper, pens, Bible

Preparation: Write either "foot," "hand," "eye," "ear," or "nose" on several index cards. Make enough cards for the number of students you expect and divide them equally between the five body parts. Fold the cards in half.

Give each preteen one of the cards. Instruct kids not to look at them. Say: **Written on your card is one of five body parts. When I say "go," look at your card and do something that will alert others who have the same word written on their cards. There is, of course, a catch. You can't make noise and you can't point to the body part. When you find a person who has the same body part, stay together and try to find everyone who has the same word. When you think you've found everyone, sit down.**

If you have a small group, don't use one or two of the suggested body parts.

When groups are formed, hand each group a piece of paper and a pen. Ask the groups to think of three things their assigned body parts do for the whole body. After several minutes have each group share its ideas with the large group. Ask:

• **What happens if one part of your body stops working?**

Say: **The Apostle Paul says in the New Testament that the church is like our bodies. Everyone is important to the church and if someone doesn't do his or her job, the whole church doesn't work as well.**

Read 1 Corinthians 12:14-20 aloud. ◼

TWO HANDS ARE BETTER THAN ONE
two hands are
better than one

Topic Connections: You can use this game to teach about cooperation or our need for others.

Game Overview: This tasty game helps preteens under--stand the importance of working together and helping each other.

Energy Level: Medium

Supplies: Napkins, oranges, peanut butter, crackers, plastic knives, resealable plastic bags

Preparation: Put several tablespoons of peanut butter into each resealable plastic bag; each pair will need one bag.

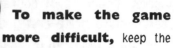

Have kids find partners, stand next to their partners, and lock arms. Explain that for the next ten minutes, everyone must stay with their partners and may only use their free hands in anything they do. Have each pair come to you to get an orange, a plastic knife, two napkins, four crackers, and the plastic bag of peanut butter.

TIP

To make the game more difficult, keep the peanut butter in the jar and have pairs use a plastic knife to get it out.

Direct each pair to peel its orange and make peanut-butter-and-cracker sandwiches. Give kids encouragement as they help each other prepare the snacks.

When kids finish making the snacks, invite them to sit on the floor in a large group. While they're enjoying the snack, ask the following questions.

• **What was it like to prepare the snack with only one hand?**

• **How did your partner help you prepare the snack?**

• **What would have happened if your partner didn't cooperate in helping you make the snack?**

When kids finish responding to the questions, remind them that it's important for people to work together if they want to get things done. Then invite them to work together to clean up. ◼

"THAT'S ME" UPSET
"that's me" upset

Topic Connections: You can use this game to teach kids about fitting in or to get them to start thinking about their unique attributes.

Game Overview: This game, based on the old favorite Fruit Basket Upset, helps kids learn about each other.

Energy Level: High

Supplies: Chairs

Preparation: Set chairs in a circle so you have one less chair than kids. Invite kids to sit in the chairs and pick one preteen to stand in the middle of the circle.

Tell kids that the person in the middle will call out characteristics that might apply to them. For example, the person in the middle might say, "Everyone wearing glasses," or "Everyone who has a brother." Then everyone to whom that characteristic applies must leave the chair and find an empty one in the circle. While this switching is taking place, the person in the middle should attempt to sit in one of the empty chairs. At the end of the rush, whoever is left without a chair becomes the next person in the middle. That person then calls out another characteristic such as, "Everyone who likes chocolate."

You may want to have the person in the middle keep their eyes closed so they can't anticipate who will be moving when they call out a certain characteristic.

If the person in the middle wants everyone in the circle to get up and change seats, then he or she should say, "That's me upset." Everyone must get up and find a new chair.

At the end of the game, ask kids what new things they learned about others in the group. ▪

CAREER CONNECTION CHARADES

career connection charades

Topic Connections: You can use this game to teach preteens about the future and the hope they have in Christ.

Game Overview: Preteens will pantomime their desired careers.

Energy Level: Medium

Supplies: Timer

Preparation: None

Gather kids into a large group. Tell them to take a minute to think about what career they'd like to have when they're older and how they can communicate what that career is without using words.

Divide the group into teams of five. Ask a volunteer from the first team to act out his or her career choice for the team. If the team does not correctly guess the profession within thirty seconds, ask the volunteer to tell the team what he or she was acting out. Repeat this process with the next team. Give everyone on each team a chance to act out his or her career goal. Then ask:

- **Why do you want to spend your time doing the career you acted out?**
- **How could you serve God in that profession?**
- **Are you hopeful about your future? Why or why not?** ◨

GARBAGE HUNT
garbage hunt

Topic Connections: You can use this game to teach kids that service is fun or to be good stewards of creation.

Game Overview: Kids will participate in a garbage scavenger hunt.

Energy Level: Medium

Supplies: Garbage bags, gloves, paper, pencil

Preparation: Walk around your church grounds or a nearby park or neighborhood and make a list of all the trash you see. For every four kids in your group, make a list of garbage items they can find and collect.

Have kids form groups of four. Give each group one of the lists you prepared, a pen, at least one trash bag, and four pairs of gloves. Set a time limit and boundaries for the game. Stress that teams must stay together at all times during the game and respect the property and privacy of others they might encounter.

> **If you want kids to form lasting relationships** with each other, have them serve together. Overcoming the fear of getting started and working together to help others accelerates unity and friendship like few classroom experiences can.

When time is up, gather all the teams back to the appropriate place and ask teams to display the items they found. Congratulate each team for its hard work and for helping to keep your church grounds or neighborhood clean. If time permits, allow groups to go back out and pick up items that weren't on their lists. ■

PICTURE WHO?
picture who?

Topic Connections: You can use this game to teach about change or becoming mature in Christ.

Game Overview: This guessing game helps kids learn more about each other's past.

Energy Level: Low

Supplies: Photographs of the kids in your group when they were infants or toddlers, a bag

Preparation: A few weeks before playing this game, gather photographs of your kids when they were infants or toddlers. Either ask the kids to bring the pictures to the group meeting or ask parents to supply them for you.

Place all the photographs of the kids who are present in a bag. Have kids sit in a circle.

Choose a volunteer to begin the game. Stand with the volunteer in the center of the circle and ask the volunteer to choose a photograph out of the bag. (If the volunteer chooses his or her own picture, replace it and have him or her choose another picture.) Ask the volunteer to look closely at the picture and then try to guess which class-

If you have a very large group, you may want to form more than one circle. Make sure the photographs given to each circle match the kids sitting in that circle.

mate it pictures. The volunteer may show the picture to the group and walk around the circle comparing the picture to the faces. Allow thirty seconds for the volunteer to guess. If the volunteer guesses correctly, ask the person who was in the photo to tell one thing about him- or herself from when he or she was an infant or toddler.

If the volunteer guesses incorrectly, allow other members of the group to guess. When the correct person is guessed, ask him or her to share the one fact. Have the person in the photo become the next volunteer. Repeat the process until all the identities have been guessed. ■

BALLOON BOUNCE
balloonbounce

Topic Connections: You can use this game to teach kids about overcoming obstacles or being sensitive to people with disabilities.

Game Overview: Kids will work together to keep balloons bouncing in the air.

Energy Level: High

Supplies: Balloons, stopwatch

Preparation: Prior to the game, inflate one or more balloons.

Tell kids the object of the game is to keep the balloon in the air for as long as possible by batting it from one person in the group to another. Explain that each person in the group will have some sort of handicap. For example, one player may only be able to use one hand. Or another may have to play the game seated in a chair. Assign a handicap to each person in the group. Other handicaps include standing in one place, playing on one's knees, or keeping both hands behind one's back.

TIP If the game isn't enough of a challenge, keep piling on the handicaps. For example, if one player can't use one arm, have the student close his or her eyes also. You can also add more balloons.

Toss the balloon in the air and begin to time how long it stays in the air. When the balloon hits the floor, stop play and announce how long the group was able to keep the balloon in the air. Toss the balloon in the air again, encouraging preteens to work together to keep the balloon in the air longer.

Gather kids in a group and ask the following questions:

- How did your handicap make you feel as you played the game?
- How did you feel when someone else from the group helped you keep the balloon in the air?
- How does this game show how we need each other?

Talk with the group about how important it is to work together and help each other in order to accomplish the tasks we've been given. ◼

CHAIN GANG
chain gang

Topic Connections: You can use this game to teach kids about resourcefulness or making the most of a situation. You can also talk about how God can do a lot with the little we have.

Game Overview: Preteens will use the things they brought to your meeting to make a huge chain.

Energy Level: Medium

Supplies: None

Preparation: None

Have kids form groups of at least five people. Say: **Using items the members of your group brought to this meeting, make the longest chain possible. The only rules are that you must keep on the clothes covering your shoulders to your knees and that every item in the chain must be connected to the items on either side. For example, you can add your shoelaces, keys, and sandals to the chain. Does anyone have any questions?**

Have a few supplies like twine and shoelaces on hand just in case preteens don't bring anything with them.

Allow groups a few minutes to work. Then look to see how long each of the chains is. You can also use a tape measure to see how long the chains are. ◼

THE HUMAN MACHINE
the human machine

Topic Connections: You can use this game to teach kids that they are an important part in the body of Christ or that we all have unique talents and gifts.

Game Overview: Preteens will connect together to make a human machine.

Energy Level: Medium

Supplies: None

Preparation: None

Have all of the kids sit down. Ask one volunteer to stand in front of the group. Say: **We're going to make a human machine. Our volunteer will begin by doing any movement, sound or action he** [or she] **would like. For example, our volunteer can move his** [or her] **arm up and down and say "ping" each time he** [or she] **moves. The volunteer will have to repeat the same motion and cannot leave the spot he** [or she] **is standing at now.**

After the first volunteer gets going, another volunteer must attach to the beginning of the machine and make his or her own movements and sounds. We'll continue this process until everyone is part of the machine.

Direct volunteers to come up and join the machine until everyone is connected. ◨

THREE-LEGGED HORSE
three-legged horse

Topic Connections: You can use this game to teach kids about working together.

Game Overview: Kids will play a classic basketball shooting game with a catch.

Energy Level: Medium

Supplies: Rope, basketball, basketball hoop

Preparation: None

Have groups form pairs. Have partners tie their inside legs together. Have pairs play in a normal game of Horse according to the following rules:

• Both partners must touch the ball when shooting.

• If a pair takes a certain shot and makes a basket, each team must either do the same or "get a letter." The first team to miss the shot gets a letter.

If you have a lot of kids, don't wait until there is a clear winner. For that matter, why wait for a clear winner at all? Just end the game when preteens begin to lose interest.

• After any missed shot, the next pair is free to invent any shot it wishes.

• If a pair gets five letters, spelling H-O-R-S-E, it can no longer participate. ■

KEEP TOGETHER
keep together

Topic Connections: You can use this game to teach kids about cliques, belonging, or working together.

Game Overview: Kids will work in teams to keep a ball.

Energy Level: High

Supplies: A ball

Preparation: None

Have kids form a large circle. Have at least two preteens volunteer to be in the middle.

Have the kids in the circle try to pass the ball without allowing it to be intercepted by one of the volunteers in the middle. Have the volunteers in the middle work together to intercept the ball. If they are successful or if they cause the ball to go outside the circle, have the person who threw the ball join them.

Continue this process until all or almost all of the kids are in the middle. Repeat the game as long as preteens show interest. Ask:

• **What was it like to be on the outside? the inside?**

• **How is that similar to or different from being on the inside or outside of a group of people?**

• **How can we make sure people always feel like they're part of this group?**

You may need to add rules as the game goes along. For example, if one preteen always charges the person holding the ball and ruins the fun for everyone, you may say, "You are not allowed to guard the person holding the ball." Or if the people in the middle never intercept the ball, you may want to simply have another person join them. You may also need to say, "You can't just pass the ball back and forth with the person directly next to you."

BLANKET SLIDE
blanket slide

Topic Connections: You can use this game to teach kids about teamwork or how God carries them through difficult times.

Game Overview: Kids will complete a relay race by dragging team members around an obstacle course on a blanket.

Energy Level: High

Supplies: Old blankets, chairs, masking tape

Preparation: Arrange an obstacle course for two teams using five or six chairs. Make sure you leave enough room for the blanket to get by without hitting the chairs. Mark a starting line with masking tape.

Have kids form two teams and give each team a blanket. Demonstrate how teams are to accomplish the obstacle course.

Begin by having one person from each team sit on the team's blanket. Have the other team members grab hold of the blanket's edges. The object is for the team to pull the person on the blanket around the obstacle course and back. If team members throw the person off the blanket, they must begin again. Each time a team gets back to the starting line, a new person should jump on the blanket and the team should run the course again. Continue this process until everyone on each team has been carried through the obstacle course.

At the end of the game, discuss the following questions:

- **In what ways did you have to work as a team to complete the race?**
- **In what ways do you need other people in your life?** ◨

COLOR MY WORLD
color my world

Topic Connections: You can use this game to teach kids about conflict or working together.

Game Overview: Kids will race to color a sheet of paper then work together to combine the colors for a new hue.

Energy Level: Low

Supplies: White paper, blue and yellow crayons

Preparation: None

Have kids form pairs. Give each team one sheet of blank white paper. Give one member of each pair a blue crayon and the other a yellow crayon.

When you say "go," each participant must color as much of the paper as possible, before his or her partner colors the area. Have kids trade crayons. Then have kids work together to make their papers completely green by each one coloring over his or her first color. ◨

When I first read this game, I thought, "No way. Crayons with preteens?" But mixing the colors works well and most preteens enjoy it.

LITTLE SECRETS AND BIG DISTORTIONS

little secrets and big distortions

Topic Connections: You can use this game to teach kids about gossip or effective communication.

Game Overview: Kids will share secrets as quickly as possible.

Energy Level: Low

Supplies: None

Preparation: None

Select three volunteers and whisper a different secret to each volunteer. For example, you could whisper, "The cow has green spots," or "Inflation is just hot air." The volunteers should spread their secrets as quickly as possible by whispering them to others. The people who receive the secrets should help spread each secret by whispering it to others also.

After all three secrets appear to have disseminated throughout the group, ask preteens to share the three secrets. See if the secrets changed as they were told and retold. Ask:

• **What does this game teach us about how rumors and other false information get spread around?**

• **What does the game teach us about gossip?**

BIBLE-in-ME GAMES

T he only thing better than a good game is a good game that has a great Bible point. Your preteens will love playing these games and they'll learn important lifelong lessons as they play. Have fun learning!

IN WITH THE NEW
in with the new

Topic Connections: You can use this game to teach kids about being a new creation in Christ.

Game Overview: Kids will change in and out of dress-up clothes to symbolize that they are new creations in Christ.

Energy Level: High

Supplies: Bible, robes, dress-up clothes, large plastic trash bags

Preparation: Put four sets of clothing (hats, shirts, vests, shorts or pants, socks, and so on) in a large plastic trash bag. Make sure there is a complete set for each preteen. Have one trash bag for every group of four kids.

H ave your kids each wear old robes over their clothes then form groups of four. Have members of each team stand in a straight line. About twenty feet in front of each group, place a trash bag full of clothes.

Say: **When I say "go," I want the first person in line to run to the bag and grab something out of it without looking into it. Whatever it is, take off your robe and put it on over the clothes you already have on. When you are done, run back and tag the next person in line. That person is then to run to the bag and do the same thing. Continue until the bag is empty. There is, however, one catch. If you pull out the same type of item as you have already pulled out in a previous turn (shirt, hat, and so on), you lose your turn.** See how fast you can outfit all the members in your team with all of the items.

You may want to ask kids in advance to bring their own robes for this game, or even the dress-up clothes if you need help gathering enough.

When the game is over, read 2 Corinthians 5:17 aloud and discuss what it means to be a new creation in Christ.

Say: **Just as you took off the robe to put on your first piece of clothing, Jesus changes your heart and makes you a new person when you believe in him. It's an immediate change. However, that doesn't mean you will be perfect or that you won't make mistakes. Just as you kept adding clothes to your outfits until the game was complete, during your life you'll keep growing in your knowledge of God until someday you will be complete.** ◼

SAFE AND DRY
safeanddry

Topic Connections: You can use this game to teach preteens about the Flood or God's protection.

Game Overview: In this game, kids will experience being protected by umbrellas and will compare that activity to Noah's being saved from the Flood.

Energy Level: High

Supplies: Umbrellas, water balloons

Preparation: Fill water balloons with water.

ead kids outdoors. Form two groups. Separate the groups by about twenty feet, and draw lines that group members are not to cross. Give each member of one group a water balloon and give each member of the other group an umbrella.

Say: **The team members with the water balloons are to try to get the other team wet. The other team is to try to avoid getting wet by using the umbrellas. No one can cross the lines between you. Please be very careful to keep the umbrellas away from everyone's faces so we don't poke any eyes or scratch any faces with them.**

Have teams begin. When all water balloons have been thrown, have teams switch roles. After the second round, discuss the following questions:

• **What was it like having an umbrella to protect you?**

• **How would you have felt if you hadn't had the umbrella?**

• **Think about the story of Noah and the ark. How is the way the umbrellas protected you similar to the way God protected Noah and his family in the ark?**

• **What can we learn from the story of Noah and the ark about how God protects us when we follow him?** ■

RUN THROUGH THE WATER
r u n t h r o u g h t h e w a t e r

Topic Connections: You can use this game to teach preteens about the Israelites crossing the Red Sea.

Game Overview: Kids will run through a line of people, simulating running through the Red Sea on dry land.

Energy Level: High

Supplies: Masking tape

Preparation: Place a line of masking tape at one end of the room.

ave preteens form two lines. Have kids in each line stand shoulder to shoulder and face the other line so that there is about three yards between the two lines. Make sure the lines begin as close to the wall as possible. Place a line of masking tape a few feet from the opposite end of the room.

Say: **The object of this game is to get everyone across the tape line at the other end of the room. However, you have to do it a step at a time. When I say, "Run through the water!" the first person in each line must run between the two rows of people and get in the end of his or her line. When you're back in line and your shoulder is touching the person next to you, shout, "Run through the water!" When the next person in line hears his or her teammate yell out, that person can run to the end of the line. Continue this process until everyone on your team is across the finish line. When players cross the finish line, they may need to move away to make room for the oncoming players to cross the line.**

If you have fewer than six kids, you may want to set up rows of six or eight chairs each. The kids should take the chairs from one end of the row to the other until they get all the chairs across the finish line.

You may want to time the game and do it a second or third time to let kids try to beat their own times. When you're finished, discuss the following questions:

- **How was this game like the Israelites crossing the Red Sea?**
- **How do you think the Israelites felt when they reached the opposite side of the Red Sea?**
- **What did God do for the Israelites in this story?**
- **What has God done for you?** ■

THE LAST LAUGH
the last laugh

Topic Connections: You can use this game to teach kids about self-control, joy, or Sarah's response to God's promise that she would have a child in her old age.

Game Overview: Pairs will compete against other pairs to see which one can keep from laughing the longest.

Energy Level: Medium

Supplies: Bible, stopwatch

Preparation: none

Say: **You know sometimes it's tough not to laugh, but we have to be able to control ourselves. Let's see what kind of laugh control we have in this room.**

Have students form pairs and have each pair combine with another to make foursomes. Pairs should flip coins to decide which pair in the foursome will first try to make the other pair laugh. Set your timer for thirty seconds and have kids begin.

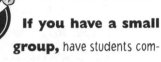

If you have a small group, have students compete individually rather than in pairs.

Students can do anything they want except touch the pair they are trying to make laugh. When both members of a pair have been made to smile (even for a second), the first round of the game is done. Have pairs switch roles and play again. Ask:

- **Was this game easy or hard for you? Why?**
- **What are some things that make you laugh?**
- **Tell of a time when you laughed the hardest—or maybe couldn't stop laughing.**

Say: **You know there was a person in the Bible who couldn't help but laugh when God said she would have a son. Let's check it out.**

Have a student read Genesis 18:9-15. Ask:

- **Why do you think Sarah had such a hard time believing God would give her a son?**

Have students form pairs and discuss the following question. Ask:

- **In what way do you most need God's help today?**

Say: **There is nothing that's too hard for God. God gave Sarah a baby in her old age. God can help us meet every challenge in our lives and satisfy any need we have.** ◼

ABRAHAM'S SERVANT RELAY
abraham'sservantrelay

Topic Connections: You can use this game to teach kids about following God, prayer, or the story of Abraham's servant finding a wife for Isaac.

Game Overview: Kids will race against time to complete a relay race.

Energy Level: High

Supplies: Bible, two buckets of water, stopwatch

Preparation: Put a bucket of water at each end of your playing area.

Open your Bible to Genesis 24. Read or summarize the passage. Then say: **Let's do a relay race to experience just a little bit of the adventure Abraham's servant experienced.**

Form the group into two equal teams. Direct one team to one side of your playing area (Point A) and the other team to the opposite side of the playing area (Point B). Let students know they'll be moving back and forth between Point A and Point B while traveling according to your directions. Explain that teams will want to go as fast as they can and that each person must go to the other point and back before the next person in line may go.

Tell kids that you will call out the mode of travel and each person must continue to travel that way until you call out a new way to move. For example, if you call out, "Kneel in a prayerful position and walk on your knees," both students who are racing should walk on their knees until you call out something else.

Call out the following directions at random:

- **Ride a "camel"** (walk on all fours).
- **Kneel in a prayerful position and walk on your knees.**
- **Carry a bucket of water** (without spilling—anyone who spills must start over).
- **Shout, dance, and clap with joy.**

- **Bow down to God** (walk or run in a bowed-down position, with fingertips touching the ground).

Time how long the relay takes to complete. Then have students try the relay several times, trying each time to beat their best time. When you have run the relay several times, lead a short discussion. Ask:

- **Which part of this relay adventure did you find most difficult? easiest?**

- **How was the relay similar to Abraham's servant's adventure?**

- **What impresses you the most about what Abraham's servant did on this mission he was on? Why?**

- **What can we learn from Abraham's servant about following God and listening to him for guidance?**

- **In what way would you like to be more like Abraham's servant?**

Say: **We must follow God closely, listening carefully to his direction to guide us. When we do, we can be confident that things will work out for God's glory.** ■

WALLS FALL DOWN
walls fall down

Topic Connections: You can use this game to teach preteens about the battle of Jericho, doing things God's way, obedience, or faith.

Game Overview: In this game, kids will attempt to get inside a circle.

Energy Level: High

Supplies: Bible

Preparation: None

Say: **Today we're going to play a game to re-enact the story of God making the walls of Jericho fall down.**

Designate half of your kids to be Walls and the other half to be Israelites. Have the Walls form a circle with the Israelites outside.

Say: **When I say "go," the Israelites are to try to get inside the cir-cle of the wall, but only two Israelites at a time can attempt to enter** the walls. The Walls are to try to keep the Israelites out. The Israelites can't run or jump at the Walls. They must get in by nudging their way through or creating a diversion.

Allow kids to play, having pairs take turns trying to get through. If some Israelites manage to get in, have the Walls reset, and give other Israelites a try. Allow the game to go on for a couple of minutes, then have teams switch roles.

Read aloud Joshua 6:15-17, 20. Have the Israelite group re-enact the Bible story and the Wall group fall to the floor when the Israelites shout out.

Say: **If the Israelites had tried to get into Jericho on their own strength, many of them probably would have died in the battle. God's way may be beyond our understanding, but it is always better in the long run.** Ask:

- **What are some things that are hard to do God's way?**
- **Why is it so important to do things God's way?** ◧

PHONE BOOK FOLLY
phone book folly

Topic Connections: You can use this game as an introduction to the story of Samson, or you can use it to teach kids about working together, wisdom, or problem-solving.

Game Overview: In this game, students will attempt to tear a phone book in half individually and then discover how they can tear it in half by working as a team.

Energy Level: Medium

Supplies: Old phone books

Preparation: None

Say: **We're going to have a phone-book-ripping contest.**

Hold up a phone book and say: **Let's see who can rip this phone book in two.**

Make phone books available to the kids and give each preteen one chance to rip a phone book in half.

After everyone has tried, say: **I guess none of us is strong enough** to tear a phone book in half. But I have an idea.

Without saying anything, slowly begin tearing the phone book into sections around an eighth of an inch thick. When you have it all torn into sections, hand a section to each participant. Say: **Don't do anything with your section until I tell you to.**

When all sections are distributed, say: **Now let's tear this phone book in half!**

When the phone book is ripped in half, cheer and celebrate! Then ask:

• **Remember Samson? Do you think Samson could have ripped this phone book in half by himself? Why or why not?**

• **Where did Samson get his power?**

• **Where did we get the power to rip the book?**

• **How is what we did like what Samson could have done?**

Say: **God gave Samson special strength to do the things he did. But he also gives us strength to do the things we need to do. Besides that, he gives us each other. If we work together in serving God, we can do mighty things for God too!** ◼

WHO WANTS TO BE A SOLOMON?

Topic Connections: You can use this game to teach kids about wisdom or to introduce Solomon.

Game Overview: In this game, teams will try to achieve levels of wisdom by answering questions.

Energy Level: Low

Supplies: Question cards from a trivia game such as Trivial Pursuit or a Bible trivia game

Preparation: Choose questions for this game in advance from the game cards you have. It's best to use only multiple-choice questions.

This game should be played similarly to the TV game show *Who Wants to Be a Millionaire?* only kids work toward becoming a Solomon instead of a millionaire. Kids can ask for one of the following lifelines any time they want to: They can have their team vote on any answer, they can ask one person from the team to give an answer, or they can have you eliminate two of the incorrect answers. Try to start with easy questions and make them harder as kids work their way up.

Have kids form teams of four to six, and have teams go through their ten questions one team at a time. Team members should take turns being in the "hot seat" question by question. Try to keep them working on doing their best, not on doing better than another team. Try to help the teams get to high levels by giving subtle or overt clues if necessary. Have teams work toward the following levels of wisdom:

Question 1: Wiser than some

Question 2: Not too bad

Question 3: Wise Old Owl

Question 4: The Thinker

Question 5: Abe Lincoln

Question 6: Aristotle

Question 7: Jeopardy winner

Question 8: Philosophy professor

Question 9: Nobel prize for wisdom

Question 10: Solomon!

When all of the teams have gone through ten questions, discuss the following:

• **The Bible tells us that Solomon was the world's wisest man. Where did his wisdom come from?**

• **Where can we get wisdom if we need it?**

• **Are you wise?**

• **How can you become wiser?** ◧

TOUCH THE KING
touchtheking

Topic Connections: You can use this game to introduce the story of Esther, to teach kids about courage, or to start a discussion about what it means to take a stand for what they believe in.

Game Overview: Students will try to be first to reach the king in this run-and-freeze game.

Energy Level: High

Supplies: Bible, crown fashioned from paper or card stock

Preparation: Consider playing this game outside. If you must remain indoors, move all furniture from the center of the room.

Say: **In Esther's time, no one dared approach the king unless summoned. People who came before the king without being called were usually killed. Let's see who can be first to touch the king without being caught and punished!**

This game is similar to Red Light, Green Light. Select the student with the shortest hair to begin the game as king (or queen). This person should stand at one end of your room or game area, wearing the paper crown you provide. Everyone else in the group is the king's royal subject who will try to be first to approach him.

They must stand at the opposite end of the room from the king, behind a start line. The king will turn his back on his subjects and say, "Come hither, and thither, one, two, three!" His subjects will race toward him as he says this, but will freeze in place before he finishes his statement. Right after his statement, the king will quickly reel around and face his subjects. Anyone the king sees who is not absolutely frozen, moving in any way (besides blinking and breathing), must return to the start line.

Keep playing this game until one of the subjects reaches the king. That subject becomes the new king if you want to play more rounds.

Summarize Esther 3–7 for students. Then lead a short discussion:

• **What kind of person do you think Esther was?**
• **Why would she risk her life for her people like this?**

• What would you have done in her situation?

• Tell us of a time when you had to choose whether or not to take a tough stand for your beliefs, stand up for someone who had been wronged, or stand up to an enemy.

• What can we learn from Esther's stand?

Say: **Esther was willing to lay down her life for her people—out of sheer love for them and God. Her stand required courage, strength, boldness, and confidence. No matter what you face in life, God stands ready to give you the courage, strength, boldness, and confidence you need to stand for him.** ◼

bustin' loose from the lions' den

Topic Connections: You can use this game to introduce the story of Daniel in the lions' den or to teach about courage.

Game Overview: Kids will try to run out of a circle without being touched by other players.

Energy Level: High

Supplies: Bibles, masking tape, stopwatch

Preparation: Tape a big circle (ten feet across) on the floor of your room for every five kids in your group.

Say: **You never know when you may get stuck in a den of lions. Right now we're going to find out what kind of busting-loose-from-the-lions'-den skills we have.**

Have students form groups of five. Each group should go and stand at a circle. Have each group choose one person to be Daniel. The other four students will be Lions. Have Daniel stand inside the circle while the Lions stand outside the circle.

Explain that Daniel will have one minute to try and flee the den without being touched by one of the Lions. To escape, Daniel must stand completely outside the circle. Have groups count how many times Daniel escapes and how many times the Lions tag him during the game. When the minute is up, have kids switch roles. Continue this process until all of the kids have had a chance to be Daniel.

Have students read Daniel 6 or summarize it for them. Ask:

• **How do you think Daniel felt when he first went into the lions' den?**

• **Tell us of a time when you felt you were surrounded by trouble or threats.**

• **What are some beliefs you have that you would die for?**

Say: **It's important to stand up for what we believe. God can give us the courage to always stand for him in every situation—even in the face of death.**

BELLY OF THE WHALE
belly of the whale

Topic Connections: You can use this game to introduce the story of Jonah. You can also take out the Jonah connection and use the game to teach kids about reaching out to others, by talking about how the fish grew in the same way the church can grow.

Game Overview: A fish will grow as it catches others.
Energy Level: High
Supplies: Bibles, blindfolds
Preparation: Move all furniture from the center of the room.

Say: **I need one volunteer to be a Fish. The rest of you will be Jonahs.**

Have students move to the center of the room. Explain that the Fish must open and close his or her mouth by putting his or her arms together then pulling them apart. The Fish should work to tag the Jonahs. Each time a Jonah is tagged, the Fish must stop while the

It may sound a little strange, but wrapping bathroom tissue around someone's eyes and head three or four times works just as well as a blindfold. It's more sanitary, and can be quickly removed.

person is blindfolded. The blindfolded person should then go in the belly of the fish by lining up behind the Fish, placing one hand on his or her shoulder, and using the other hand to try and tag those not yet captured. Continue this game until everyone has become part of the Fish.

Summarize the story of Jonah or have students read the first chapter of the book of Jonah.

Say: **Jonah thought he could escape his problem by running away—kind of like how you ran away from the Fish. But God had work for Jonah to do. In his mercy, God used the fish to bring Jonah back to Nineveh. And because of Jonah's preaching, the whole city repented and turned back to God.** Ask:

• **Why do you think Jonah ran away from God?**

• **Why do you think God went to such lengths to get Jonah to come back?**

• **Have you ever run away from God or what you thought God wanted you to do? What happened?** ◪

BALLOON BUST
balloonbust

Topic Connections: You can use this game to introduce the story of Jesus feeding the five thousand, or to talk about justice and equity. You can also talk about how "fair" Jesus' death for our sins is.

Game Overview: Kids will pop balloons to win points.

Energy Level: Medium

Supplies: Bible; balloons; white, green, and blue strips of paper; garbage bags; snacks

Preparation: Blow up two balloons for each preteen. Place one strip of colored paper in half of the balloons. Put the balloons in garbage bags for easy handling.

Have kids form groups of four. Tell kids that you are going to dump balloons on the floor. When you say go, they will begin stomping on the balloons to make them pop. Explain that they must check the balloons after they are popped because some contain strips of paper that are worth points. Tell kids that they'll have to earn a certain amount of points before they can have a snack. Dump the balloons on the floor and begin.

After all of the balloons have been popped, have the preteens return to their groups. Tell them that the white strips are worth two points, the green strips are worth four points, and the blue strips are worth six points. Have groups add up their points and tell the rest of the groups how many points they earned. Announce that they must have one or more points to win the snack, and distribute the snack to everyone.

While you are eating, ask the following questions:

• **Were you worried that you might not get a snack during this game?**

• **How did you feel when you found out everyone gets a snack?**

Read John 6:5-13. Ask:

• **How is this story similar to what happened in our game?**

Say: **Jesus used five small loaves and two small fish to feed at least five thousand people. What he had was enough. In our game, no matter how many points you had, it was enough to get a snack. Jesus can take whatever we have, no matter how small, and turn it into something wonderful.** ◨

BLIND DRAW
blind draw

Topic Connections: You can use this game to teach kids about Peter walking on the water, trust, or even service.

Game Overview: Kids will trust someone to guide them in drawing a picture.

Energy Level: Low

Supplies: Bible, blindfolds, markers, paper

Preparation: none

Have preteens form pairs. Give each pair a marker and two pieces of paper. Blindfold one person in each pair. Explain that the partner without the blindfold will tell his or her blindfolded partner what to draw by giving step-by-step directions. Gather the non-blindfolded partners in a huddle and tell them to have their partners draw a house without revealing what the final goal is.

Have kids switch roles and repeat the process. This time, direct the non-blindfolded partners to help their partners draw a sailboat.

Repeat the game. This time, have non-blindfolded kids direct their partners to draw a car (and then a shark) while holding the hand of the blindfolded partner to aid in drawing the picture. The blindfolded partners should relax their hands so the seeing partners can do the work easily.

When pairs have finished, ask them to compare pictures. Ask:

• **What was it like to draw without being able to see?**

• **Did you trust the person who was helping you draw? Why or why not?**

Read Matthew 14:25-31. Ask:

• **Why was Peter able to walk on the water?**

• **Why did he sink?**

• **How is trusting the person who helped us draw like trusting Jesus?**

Say: **When we put our faith in Jesus and let him lead our lives, we can do whatever God calls us to do. If we get caught up listening to what is going on around us, we can stumble and lose our faith. If we let Jesus guide how we live, we will experience amazing things.** ◼

FORGIVENESS FREEZE TAG
forgiveness freeze tag

Topic Connections: You can use this game to teach preteens about Jesus healing the paralytic as found in Matthew 9, about forgiveness, or about being set free.

Game Overview: Kids will play a game of Freeze Tag to learn about how Jesus frees and heals us.

Energy Level: High

Supplies: Bible, traffic cones

Preparation: Use the cones to mark off a playing field.

hoose one volunteer to be the Healer. Designate one-third of your kids to be Paralyzers, and tell the rest that they are Paralytics. Explain that the Paralytics are to make it from one end of the field to the other without being tagged by a Paralyzer. If they are tagged, they must freeze. Emphasize that the only way they can move again is to be touched by the Healer. Have the Paralytics go to one end of the field and have the Paralyzers go to the middle.

After a few rounds, gather kids together. Have a student read Matthew 9:1-8 aloud. Ask:

• **What do you think it would be like to really be paralyzed?**

• **How was the Healer in our game like Jesus?**

• **What does Jesus do for us beyond forgiving our sins?**

Say: **In this Scripture, Jesus healed the paralytic by saying, "Your sins are forgiven!" That wasn't enough for some people. They thought he was saying something he didn't have the authority to say. So Jesus said, "Get up, take your mat and go home," and the man did so. Then, the people in the crowd knew Jesus had the authority to heal sins. Jesus can heal your body. But more important, Jesus can heal your heart.** ■

I'M FREE
i'm free

Topic Connections: You can use this game to teach kids about the Resurrection or freedom in Christ.

Game Overview: Partners will try to prevent a blindfolded person from being set free.

Energy Level: High

Supplies: Tape, blindfolds

Preparation: Use masking tape to mark off an area that is big enough for your group to comfortably walk around in.

hoose a volunteer, and have him or her put on a blindfold. Form trios, and have everyone step inside the area you've designated for playing the game. Give each trio a blindfold, and ask each trio to blindfold one person in the trio. Instruct the sighted kids to face each other and hold hands. Have the blindfolded preteens stand between the two sighted preteens inside their arms.

Say: **My volunteer has been freed and is now going to help set others free. Those of you who are holding hands, it's your job to gently guide the person between your hands away from my volunteer. If my volunteer tags any of you, the two people who were holding hands must let go and move out of the playing field. The person with the blindfold who was between their arms can then try to set other people free by tagging them.**

If you go out of the playing field, help those with blindfolds stay inside it by gently guiding them back in.

Have kids begin the game and help your volunteer navigate throughout the playing area.

Once everyone is free, give kids the opportunity to switch roles and play the game again. Then ask:

- **What did it feel like to be trapped between two people's arms?**
- **How did it feel to be set free?**
- **How did Jesus set us free?**
- **How can we help set others free?** ◨

GAMES FOR LITTLE CLUSTERS OF PRETEENS

So you've got ten (or even less) preteens just *dying* for some fun. Here are eleven games in a wide range of styles: outside, inside, high-energy, low-energy (and energies in between), some prep, no prep. So try these great games with your small group of preteens and soon you'll need the Games for Big Bunches of Preteens in the next chapter!

MAILBOX RELAY!
mailbox relay!

Topic Connections: Use this game to help preteens see how the Bible can answer life's questions.

Game Overview: Players will take turns running to a mailbox, retrieving an envelope, opening it, and following the directions written inside.

Energy Level: Medium

Supplies: Two boxes with the word "mail" written across the front, paper, envelopes, pens, sticky notes, stamp pad, stamp, one-cent postage stamps

Preparation: Write out on pieces of paper specific "find-it" items or places for your players to locate. For example, you could write: "Locate where we quench our thirst" (drinking fountain), "Locate the place where we take our youngest to play and rest" (nursery), or "Locate the place where our pastor prepares his message" (pastor's office). Insert each different instruction in a different envelope. Also, stick stamps onto a sticky note and insert the stamped note into each envelope and seal. Place all the envelopes inside the mailboxes. Divide the envelopes equally between the two mailboxes.

Divide the group into small teams of five or less. Position each team's mailbox on opposite sides of the room.

Say: **When I say "go," one person from each team will run to his or her mailbox, take out an envelope, open it, and read the clue to his or her team. Once your team figures out the specified item or place, the first person will run to it and stick the postage-stamped sticky note on the item. Then bring the empty envelope back to me and I'll "cancel" it using the stamp pad. Run back to your group and sit down. Then the next player repeats the process. Keep running and retrieving envelopes until your mailbox is empty. Once all the mail has been removed, sit down in a circle and say, "Mail delivery complete!"** Ask:

• **Was it easy or hard to find your items to stamp?**

By placing the stamps on sticky notes, you'll be able to easily remove the stamps from the places the kids locate (your pastor might not appreciate postage stamps stuck on the his office door!).

To make the game easier, you could use the same stamp and stamp pad on the sticky notes as you do on the envelopes.

Instructions on the letters can also include doing simple physical tasks such as running around the room three times, doing ten push-ups, doing twenty jumping jacks. Or, each letter could give the instruction to act out a charade or even look up a particular Bible verse and recite it.

• **Were the letters inside your envelopes helpful in finding your items? Explain.**

Say: **In our game, you had to guess where you needed to go. But God doesn't make us guess.** Ask:

• **How can the Bible help you find answers to life's questions?**

Have teams race to retrieve their sticky notes and see which team finishes first. ◻

FINGER TWIST
finger twist

Topic Connections: Use this game to teach about thinking before acting.

Game Overview: Preteens will match the numbers written on their fingers to other team members' to complete a simple math problem.

Energy Level: Medium

Supplies: Pens

Preparation: Prepare a list of simple math problems to call out. For example, "When you add these two numbers together, you get the number fifteen" or "When you subtract these two numbers, you get the number four."

Instruct every player to write the numbers 1 to 10 on their fingers so that each finger has a different number written on it. Form two teams. Players should stand in a group awaiting your instructions. Each group must figure out a math problem you pose, then two players should "stick" the appropriate numbered fingers together.

Not every player will stick to another teammate each time you call out an instruction. However, at least two people on the team must "stick" fingers every time. After a few math problems have been called out, both teams' hands will be in pretzel-like shapes as kids try to find available fingers to complete the problem.

Say: **Move into a circle with your team. When I call out a math problem, solve it by figuring out what two numbers you need. One player should "stick" the appropriate finger number to a second team member's finger. Don't unstick your fingers until the game is over. I will keep calling out instructions until one team is unable to complete the direction. Remember, there will be more than one solution to each problem.**

Continue giving directions until one team isn't able to match numbered fingers in answer to your math question.

Say: **Sometimes we think following instructions is going to be easy...and it isn't.** Ask:

• **When was a time you thought a project or an assignment looked simple but it turned into a disaster because you didn't know what you were getting into?**

• **What are some situations you face where you need to think before acting?**

• **God's Word tells us to think before we act. What are some practical ways we can learn to do this?** ◨

PICTURES INTO WORDS

Topic Connections: Use this game to teach about honest and open communication.

Game Overview: Players will translate key words of a Bible verse into pictures for other preteens to figure out.

Energy Level: Low

Supplies: Bible, chalkboard, chalk, index cards

Preparation: Write out numerous Bible verses on separate index cards for players to use in their sketches on the board. Examples could include Exodus 14:21 and Matthew 7:24-27. Circle the words you expect the players to illustrate on the board.

Words such as the, it, is, and, but, whomever, and thou are difficult to capture in a picture. It helps to select verses with people, animals, food, and other tangible objects for players to draw.

Divide preteens into two teams of five or less. Hand out one card to each team. Allow a few minutes for teams to discuss how to best illustrate their verses on the board. When ready, have one team go to the board and begin drawing word pictures for every circled word on their card. They can write the remaining words in the appropriate spaces between their pictures. When finished, the other group must try to guess the verse depicted. Then repeat the process with the second team. Continue handing out new verses and writing them out as long as time permits.

Following the game, ask:

• **Was it easy or hard figuring out the verses in this game?**

• **When was a time you had trouble understanding what someone meant when he or she said something?**

• **God expects us to speak the truth in love, which means speaking in a loving, respectful way. How can we learn to be better communicators?** ◼

PROSTHETIC NOSES
prostheticnoses

Topic Connections: Use this crazy contest for an unforgettable object lesson on being honest with who we are.

· ·

Game Overview: Participants will create new noses out of Silly Putty.

Energy Level: Low

Supplies: Mirrors, Silly Putty

Preparation: Gather the necessary items. Consider making a certificate for the contest winner by cutting pictures of noses from magazines and taping them to a page that reads, "Best Prosthetic Nose Award."

Make mirrors available to participants and distribute the Silly Putty.

Say: **Give yourself a nose job using these supplies.**

Students should then go to work molding the putty on their noses to create a new look!

Afterward, ask players to vote for the nose they like best. Ask:

Chewed chewing gum could be used as an economical, albeit offensive, substitute for Silly Putty.

• **What was it like creating new noses for yourselves?**

• **How do these noses create a false representation of your face?**

• **What are other ways you portray a "false image" of yourself?**

Say: **It can be fun creating new noses as we did. But it's easy to create a false image of ourselves in other ways. We all need to remember God wants us to be honest with who we really are, both to others and ourselves. After all, God made each of us and values us all equally.** ◼

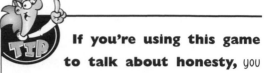

If you're using this game to talk about honesty, you might want to also show the clip from *Pinocchio* where his nose grows as he tells lies. Then discuss how lying is another way we present a false self to others.

LIMA BEAN PASS
limabeanpass

Topic Connections: Use this game to teach about getting stuck in unhealthy habits.

Game Overview: Participants will try to pass lima beans down a row wearing sticky gloves.

Energy Level: Medium

Supplies: Latex rubber gloves, spray adhesive, large bowls, trash bags, dried lima beans

Preparation: Collect needed supplies. Place the lima beans in big bowls, one for each team.

Consider playing this game outdoors since it could be messy.

To begin, pass out latex gloves and have each student put on a pair. Divide the group into two teams of equal size, and ask each team to form a line. At one end of the line, place a giant bowl of lima beans. At the other end of the line, place a large empty bowl.

For extra fun, cook the beans!

Next, go down each row and spray all the gloves with aerosol adhesive until they are sticky. Say: **When I say "go," the first person in line should grab lima beans from the bowl and begin passing them down** the line. The last person in each row should deposit the beans in the empty bowl next to him or her.

Begin the game. Have trash bags nearby for easy cleanup. Ask:

• **Did you think this game would be easy or hard? Explain.**

• **The adhesive made the beans hard to get off your hands. How are the beans sticking to** our hands like getting stuck in unhealthy habits?

• **How can God help you avoid unhealthy habits?**

Say: **Just as it was hard to keep the beans from sticking to your hands, it can be hard to choose healthy habits. Let's remember to always look to God for help.** ■

Be careful when using the aerosol adhesive. Use adequate ventilation and avoid spraying skin with the adhesive.

Q-TIP GOLF
q-tip golf

Topic Connections: This is just a fun game for preteens to play. However, you could use this game to discuss trying to do your best.

Game Overview: Participants will shoot cotton swabs through straws toward nine goals around the room.

Energy Level: Medium

Supplies: Straws, cotton swabs, brightly colored paper, stickers, tape, pens, "Golf Score Card" handouts

Preparation: Ahead of time, number paper signs 1 through 9 and use tape to hang them in various spots around the room or playing area. Make a photocopy of the "Golf Score Card" handout (page 55) for every two players and cut them apart for each player.

Be sure to check the size of your straws before the game. Some straws won't allow the cotton swabs to pass through easily.

o begin, give each participant a cotton swab and a straw. Provide stickers and ask players to place a sticker on the shaft of their swab so they will be able to identify it as their own.

Next, hand out pens and score cards, and say: **Blow the cotton swab through your straw toward the first sign. If you don't hit the sign on the first try, you must shoot your swab a second time from the place where it landed.**

You may want to have kids stand about six feet from the goals, but try out your combination of straws and cotton swabs to determine the best distance for your materials.

Continue until you have hit the sign completing the first hole. Then record on your score card the number of tries it took. Move on to the second sign, and so forth. Goals must be completed in numbered order.

Play the game as you would miniature golf, alternating turns in an orderly way. ■

ONE SHOT AT A TIME
one shot at a time

Topic Connections: Use this game to explore the truth of everyone being important on a team.

Game Overview: Kids will play a basketball game where everyone gets to shoot.

Energy Level: High

Supplies: Basketball, basketball hoop

Preparation: None

orm teams of no more than five. For each team designate the shooter (preferably someone customarily shy or unassertive). The designated shooter should change with each possession. Conduct the game according to normal basketball rules except that

• each score counts one point,

• all teams shoot for the same basket with no need to "take it back" when possession changes, and

GOLF SCORE CARD

HOLE	PAR	SCORE
1		
2		
3		
4		
5		
6		
7		
8		
9		

HOLE	PAR	SCORE
1		
2		
3		
4		
5		
6		
7		
8		
9		

• only the designated shooter for that possession can score.

Play the game up to twenty points. Then discuss the uniqueness of this version of the game. Ask:

• **How was this game different from other team games you've played?**

• **Did you enjoy this game more or less than other team games?**

• **Did you get to be more or less involved in this game compared to other team games?**

• **How did that make you feel?**

Say: **Often, a star player gets the time and attention in games. The fact that many games are "team games" gets lost in these situations. But our game was designed to see that everyone is important. You may not be a gifted athlete, but God has gifted each of us in unique ways.** ■

WHO? WHAT? HOW?
who? what? how?

Topic Connections: Use this game to build communication skills.

Game Overview: This silly mix 'n' match guessing game is good for small groups to build communication skills.

Energy Level: Medium

Supplies: Index cards, pens or pencils

Preparation: None

Give everyone three index cards and a pen or pencil. Tell your pre-teens to each write on one of the index cards the name of a favorite cartoon character or popular TV character. When everyone is finished, collect those index cards and put them in a pile.

On the second card, have everyone write an occupation. Encourage kids to be creative; they might write down a rutabaga farmer, an encyclopedia salesman, a lollipop maker, or a dog trainer. When everyone is finished, collect those index cards and put them in a pile.

Then tell your kids to each write on another index card something silly that might be used as a mode of transportation—a riding lawn mower, a giant teacup, a baby stroller, a rolling log, a pelican, a bathtub, or a cloud, for example. When everyone is finished, collect those index cards and put them in a third pile.

Tell kids that they are going to participate in a role-play. Shuffle the cards in the first pile and pass one to each person, making sure no one else sees the cards. Then shuffle the second pile and distribute them. Shuffle the third pile, and distribute them. It's OK if some kids get the same cards that they wrote on. Have kids line up on one side of the room.

Have the first person in line go first.

Tell that person he or she must act out the character on the card, the job listed on the second card, and the mode of transportation on the third card. While that person begins the role-play, the next person in line will "drive" up next to the first person, acting out the character, occupation, and transportation on his or her cards.

The second person will ask the first person, "Who are you?" The first person will act out his or her character and reply with some sort of clue as to who he or she is without repeating any of the words that are on the index cards. So, for example, if the first person's character is Bugs Bunny, he or she might say, "What's up, Doc? Got a carrot?"

Then the second person will ask the first person, "What do you do?" The first person will act out his or her occupation and give a clue without repeating any of the words that are on the index cards. So, for example, if "Bugs Bunny" selected "encyclopedia salesman," he or she might say, "Say, Doc, would you like to buy some reference books?"

Then the second person will ask, "How do you get to work?" and the first person will act out according to the occupation on the card. So, for example, if "Bugs Bunny" selected "riding on a pelican," he or she might say, "Let me tell you, Doc, this bird can really fly—and my luggage fits in his beak!"

After the three questions have been asked and the first person has had a chance to reply, the second person tries guessing the first person's "who," "what," and "how." If he or she doesn't guess correctly, the first person can say the "who," "what," and "how," and then sit down.

Then the next person will "drive" up to the second person and ask him or her the same three questions.

Play until all the kids have had a chance to role-play their situations. ◪

THE POWER OF ONE
the power of one

Topic Connections: Use this game to teach about peer pressure and not going along with the crowd.

Game Overview: Kids will bounce numbered balls through a hole in a sheet.

Energy Level: Medium

Supplies: A sheet or blanket, small balls (such as tennis balls), scissors, black marker, name tags

Preparation: In the center of the bedsheet, cut a hole that is slightly larger than the diameter of the balls being used. Number the balls and assign one to each person. Put corresponding numbers on the name tags and hand them out together with the balls. Lay the bedsheet on the floor.

Give each preteen a ball, and have them all gather around the sheet. Then have kids place their numbered balls in the sheet. Next, have kids grab the edge of the sheet with both hands and, when told to start, begin pumping the sheet up and down. This action keeps the balls bouncing in the air and allows them to fall through the hole in the sheet, one at a time. See which preteen's numbered ball stays on the sheet. Play multiple rounds if time permits.

If necessary, guide the kids toward discussing any dangerous or immoral activities they may face, such as drinking alcohol, smoking tobacco, doing drugs, stealing, or engaging in sexual sins.

After the game ends, ask the kids to gather around for a discussion.

Say: **There is a lesson here. We all like to get along with our friends and do things together. However, in the ups and downs of life, there are times when it's important for us not to go along with the crowd. If we do, we might wind up like most of these balls did and just fall through the holes that are out there in the real world. There are times when the winner in real life is the one who does not go along with the crowd.** Ask:

• **In what types of activities should we avoid just going along with the crowd?**

- What should we not do even if our friends want to?
- How can we say "no" and yet still be with our friends? ▪

CARD CREATIVITY
card creativity

Topic Connections: Use this game to help preteens express their creativity.

Game Overview: Kids will think up new ways to organize playing cards.

Energy Level: Low

Supplies: Several decks of cards

Preparation: Shuffle the decks of cards into one big deck.

Have kids sit in a circle around the expanded deck of cards. Explain to kids that they'll quickly pass the cards around the circle, one at a time, until each player has six cards. The object is for each person to choose a creative way to organize the cards, such as all cards being the same suit, or three of one number and three of one suit. After kids have their six cards, they can draw one card at any time to help them create their desired card pattern. When a player draws a card, he or she must also discard one face-down in the center of the circle—and these cards may be used by other players.

This game is designed to stretch kids' creative abilities. However, if you find six cards is too much of a challenge, decrease the number to five or four.

When a player has his or her desired order, he or she should say "stop," and display the card pattern. Once a pattern has been created, it cannot be repeated by the other players. Play until everyone has run out of ideas for card patterns. After the game, ask:

- **What was harder, trying to think of creative card patterns or trying to get the cards you needed to make those patterns?**
- **Did you stick with your original plan or did new cards give you fresh ideas? Explain.**
- **How did this game give you ideas of how to think creatively about solving problems you're facing?** ▪

section **five**

GAMES FOR BIG BUNCHES OF PRETEENS

There's a sea of preteens out there and they're getting restless. They're starting to wrestle, argue, and break things. Quick! Use some of these games for large groups of twenty or more kids before you're swept under the wave.

SNOW In SEPTEMBER
snowinseptember

Topic Connections: This is a fun game that can also be used to demonstrate teamwork.

Game Overview: Teams will throw paper "snowballs" at each other.

Energy Level: High

Supplies: Paper, watch

Preparation: none

Have preteens form two teams, and have teams gather at opposite ends of the room. Declare the middle area of the room "off limits." Give each team stacks of scrap paper.

Say: **Wow! It's snowing inside! Let's have an indoor snowball game. Use the paper to make snowballs, and then throw the snowballs into the other team's territory. You can also deflect incoming snowballs, but only by batting** at them with your open hand. Once a snowball lands, you can't touch it. You'll play for three minutes, and then we'll count how many snowballs made it into enemy territory.

If necessary, you may want to switch a few players between teams to even the scoring during the game.

Start the game, and call "time" after three minutes have passed. Have each team count the snowballs in its territory. Play several rounds.

If there's real snow outside, play the game outside. Have some towels handy to dry the hands of kids who forgot to bring gloves.

After several rounds, gather kids and ask:

• **How did working as teammates help you do better in this game?**

• **What are other ways teamwork helps you to do better in life?**

• **How can you be a better teammate?** ■

ASSEMBLY WORKERS
a s s e m b l y w o r k e r s

Topic Connections: Use this game to let preteens have fun expressing their creative ability.

Game Overview: Players will work together to create a descriptive scene from a Bible story using decorative food items.

Energy Level: Low

Supplies: Bibles, tables, paper plates, napkins, knives, baked pan-sized cookies, frosting, decorating supplies

Preparation: Select several Bible stories which are colorful and exciting for the preteens to re-create on their pan-sized cookies. Examples include animals entering the ark, Joseph and his many-colored coat, and Moses leading the Israelites from Egypt. Write these story titles on separate pieces of paper. Set up long tables for an assembly line using assorted decorating items. You'll need one table, pan cookie, and decorating ingredients for every twenty preteens.

Divide large group into teams of ten to twenty kids each. Hand out one story title to each group. Have groups choose a Bible reader to read or summarize the stories. Then allow a few minutes for groups to plan how to best depict their story using items such as frosting, decorating tubes, sprinkles, candies, nuts, coconut, or marshmallows. When ready, have each group line up in an assembly-line fashion on opposite sides of the long table. Each player should have some kind of decorative food item to work with as the group's cookie pan will make its way down the table.

Say: **Line up with your teammates and get ready to decorate your cookie. The players opposite of each other at the front of the table will begin decorating. Each opposite pair will have fifteen seconds to decorate before the pan is passed to the next pair. When the pans get to the end of the table, we'll stop and look at what our cookie assembly line created!**

Begin the game, calling out time every fifteen seconds. When the pans have reached the end of the tables, have the other teams try to guess the story depicted. If no one can guess, send the pan down the assembly line again, using the above process.

For a greater challenge, you could use submarine sandwich ingredients. Start with long bread halves and use various sub sandwich ingredients to create the stories.

Once teams have guessed each other's Bible stories, hand out paper plates and napkins, cut the cookies into bars, and enjoy. Ask:

• **In what ways were parts of this game frustrating? Explain what you felt when you realized you had to work fast.**

• **How does God feel about rushing through our responsibilities?**

• **Whatever we do, the Bible says we should do it as if working for Christ. What are some ways we can be sure we are giving him our very best?** ◼

STATIONARY SOCCER
stationary soccer

Topic Connections: This silent game could be used to talk about finding God's direction or knowing God's will. It also works as a subtle clumpbreaker game.

Game Overview: Teams will compete to get their blindfolded "soccer ball" player through a goal.

Energy Level: Low

Supplies: Blindfolds

Preparation: None

You'll need at least thirty kids and a large area to play this game. Have kids form teams of ten to fifteen. Have teams choose one player to be the human soccer ball and give him or her a blindfold. Have the remaining kids in each team spread out in a bowling-pin pattern. If you have fifteen players, start the point of the pin pattern using two kids standing about four feet apart. Then have a second row of three kids stand four feet from the first row, and four feet apart from each other. Continue with this spacing for the third row of four kids, and the fourth row of five kids. If you have fewer kids on each team, decrease rows or number of kids in each row.

Blindfold each human soccer ball, and lead him or her to stand somewhere between the third and fourth rows (or in the middle of the longer rows if you have smaller teams). Spin each soccer ball a few times, and then say: **The object of this game is for the blindfolded human soccer ball to score a goal by walking between the two goalpost players in the first row. No one may talk, but if your soccer ball is going to bump into you, you can try to spin him or her toward the right direction. You can touch only your soccer ball's arms or shoulders, and only for one second. If you touch your soccer ball anywhere else or for longer than one second, he or she has to start from the beginning.**

Answer any questions preteens may have about the game before enforcing the silent rule as the game is played.

Say: **This is a silent game. From now on, everyone must be completely silent.**

Play several rounds, having teams choose a new soccer ball with each round. After the last round is finished, ask the kids to gather around, and ask the human soccer balls:

• **Was it hard knowing where to go? Why or why not?**

Ask everyone:

• **When are times you have a hard time knowing what to do?**

• **How can God give you direction when you need it?** ◪

HUMAN ESCALATOR
human escalator

Topic Connections: Use this game to teach about bearing one another's burdens.

Game Overview: Preteens will use towels as chairs to carry players to the head of the line.

Energy Level: Medium

Supplies: Towels

Preparation: None

You'll need twenty kids to form two teams. Add more teams for larger groups. Have kids form teams of ten, and have each team form a single-file line. Give the first preteen in each line a towel. Say: **When I give the signal, the first player in each line will pass the towel over his or her head to the next player. The next player will repeat the same action, and again until the towel is at the end of the line. When the towel reaches the last player in line, the two players just ahead in line will quickly drop back, grab the ends of the towel, and carry the person to the head of the** line. The closest person in line will follow the carried person, acting as a spotter. Finally, the carried person will again pass the towel backward over his or her head, as the towel gets passed down the line.

Give a signal to start the game, and have teams play until everyone has been carried in the towel "escalator" and the original first player is back in position. Play several rounds of the game. ◼

TANGLED UP IN FRIENDSHIPS
tangledupinfriendships

Topic Connections: Use this game to discuss friendships or the importance of names.

Game Overview: Preteens will learn names while linking themselves together with yarn.

Energy Level: Low

Supplies: Skein of yarn

Preparation: None

Have preteens sit in a circle. Say: **Our names are important. We're going to play a game that will help us see this. I want each person to say your name loudly. Then we all will say "hello" to this person using his or her name.**

After everyone has greeted each other, explain that you want preteens to say their names again. But this time kids will also share their favorite hobby. For example, someone might say, "My name is Sara and I like horseback riding." The group then will respond, "Hello Sara. You like horseback riding."

Show kids the skein of yarn. Have one person tie the yarn to his or her wrist. Say: **Everyone has heard each other's name and favorite hobby. [Name] will begin by saying either a person's name or hobby. When you hear your name or hobby, hold up your hand so the yarn can be tossed to you. When you catch the yarn, wrap it around your wrist a few times. We'll keep saying names or hobbies until everyone is holding the yarn. If you are called by your name, then say your hobby when you catch the yarn. If you are called by your hobby, then say your name.**

Have kids repeat the process, each time tossing the yarn to someone new. If kids forget names or hobbies, have a volunteer on the opposite side of the circle say his or her name and hobby again. Keep the game moving until everyone has caught the yarn.

After the game, ask the group to look at the tangled web of yarn. Ask:

• **How is this pattern of yarn like friendship?**

• **How does it feel to be a part of this yarn web?**

• **Why are friendships important?** ▪

SING ME A SONG!

Topic Connections: Use this game to help preteens see their need for each other.

Game Overview: Kids will put together lyrics to popular songs, and then sing the songs.

Energy Level: Medium

Supplies: Index cards, marker

Preparation: Choose several songs that kids will know, such as "The Star-Spangled Banner," "Jesus Loves Me," and "Happy Birthday to You." If you want the game to be a bit more challenging, choose songs that may be a little less familiar. Write one phrase of a song on each index card; for example, on one card, you might write, "O say can you see." You'll need one card for each person.

This game works best for groups of twenty to thirty. For larger groups, you'll just need to choose more songs and make more lyric cards. You could also repeat some of the songs and the cards for quicker preparation time.

Give each person an index card. Tell preteens that they'll need to mingle and find others in the group who have the rest of the phrases of their songs. When they've completed their songs, have them form groups according to the songs they have. Ask:

• **Was it easy or hard finding people with the phrases to your song?**

- How did having all the words to your song help make the song complete?
- How did this game help you see how you need each other?

Then explain that their next task is to entertain the group with rousing renditions of their songs. Encourage each group to really "ham up" its performance of the song. Give groups some time to practice, and then hold an "instant talent show."◼

WHO'S MOLDING YOU?
who's molding you?

Topic Connections: Use this game to help preteens see the importance of being shaped by God.

Game Overview: Preteens will run relays with clay objects.

Energy Level: High

Supplies: Clay

Preparation: None

You'll need a large area for this game. Have preteens form groups of five or six. Give each group a lump of clay. Say: **The Bible talks about God being the potter and we're the clay. In your groups, I want you to mold your clay into some symbol representing what you think God would want you to be.**

After kids have made their objects, have groups line up in relay teams. Have groups run a circular relay (like running around an oval track), using the group's clay object as a baton. After the game, ask:

- How did your group's clay symbol get changed using it as a baton?
- The Bible says we need to let God mold us. How is the way we handled the clay during the relay like the way we mold ourselves?
- What is some way you need God to mold you?◼

I'VE GOT RHYTHM!

I've got rhythm!

Topic Connections: This game is just for fun, but you might use it to illustrate concentration.

Game Overview: Kids will demonstrate their rhythm skills in this large-group game.

Energy Level: Low

Supplies: none

Preparation: none

Have kids sit in a circle and number off; each person should be assigned his or her own number. Be sure to include yourself in the numbering. Get kids started with this simple rhythm: slap their knees twice, clap their hands twice, snap their left hand fingers then their right hand fingers. Have kids repeat the rhythm together several times.

Then explain that you'll start the game by saying your own number on the first snap and someone else's number on the second snap. The person whose number you called will need to say his or her number on the first snap and another number on the next snap. The challenge is to keep the rhythm going and say numbers on each set of snaps.

Continue in this manner until everyone has had a chance to say numbers. ◼

QUIET GAMES

reteens love action. But they also need times to cool down. These games offer a variety of ways for preteens to stretch their brains, express their creativity, and enhance their communication skills—all while having fun (the *essential* preteen ingredient!).

ART RELAY RACE
a r t r e l a y r a c e

Topic Connections: Use this game to teach cooperation skills.

Game Overview: Preteens will each contribute to drawing a group picture.

Energy Level: Low

Supplies: newsprint, crayons, tables, stopwatch

Preparation: none

ivide the group into two equal teams. Give each team a piece of newsprint and crayons. Select an event or theme to be the main topic of both pictures. For example, you could choose an amusement park, downtown scene, baseball game, or popular Bible story such as the Exodus crossing.

Say: **Each member on your team will have thirty seconds to draw a part of the picture. After thirty seconds, I'll say "pass," and the next person will have his or her chance to draw.**

Announce the picture topic and have the first player on each team begin drawing. After thirty seconds, signal the next person to begin his or her contribution to the picture. After the picture has made the rounds to each person, ask:

- **How do the portions of each picture reflect the chosen theme?**
- **How did each new part of the picture help you know what to draw?**
- **We cooperated with each other drawing these pictures. What are some other ways we can cooperate with each other?** ◼

CLAY FRIENDSHIPS
clay friendships

Topic Connections: Use this game to show the importance of relationships.

Game Overview: Teams will make interlocking clay chains.

Energy Level: Low

Supplies: Modeling clay

Preparation: None

Form teams of three or four. Give each team member a small piece of clay. Have team members roll their pieces of clay into snake-like shapes. Say: **Each team will race to build a chain using the pieces of clay. One team member will make a link out of clay and the next person will link his or her clay, forming a chain. If your link breaks, you must fix it before continuing. The last person on your team needs to keep his or her link open, because each team's chain will need to be linked to another team's chain.**

Have teams begin building chains. After teams are all linked together in a large chain loop, say: **You all worked together to build your chains and loop them together.** Ask:

- **How did you help each other make a chain that held together?**
- **How is this like friends helping each other?** ◧

WHAT'S IN A WORD?
what's in a word?

Topic Connections: Use this game to demonstrate problem-solving skills.

Game Overview: Preteens will work to strategically eliminate letters while creating words.

Energy Level: Low

Supplies: A room with several windows, canned "snow," paper, pencils, damp cloth

Preparation: On each window, write the word "snowing" with the canned snow.

Have your preteens form the same number of groups as you have windows.

Say: **One day, when it was _really_ hot, a person wrote the word "snowing" on a window, because he wanted to think about something cold. Then he rubbed out one letter and discovered a new word. He rubbed out another letter and realized he still had a new word. He kept doing this, until he had only one letter left, and that was also a word.**

As a team, work out the order in which he erased the letters and what words he created. Have one person on your team be the recorder and write down your team's answers.

The solution:

n	Sowing	**G**	Sin
o	Swing	**S**	In
w	Sing	**n**	I

After the game, ask:

- **Was it easy or hard to find the solution?**
- **How did you work together as a team to solve the puzzle?**
- **How can teamwork help you in other areas?** ▪

BLIND BUILDING
blind building

Topic Connections: This game could be used to learn about communication skills.

Game Overview: Preteens will use verbal skills as partners describe and build a Lego building.

Energy Level: Low

Supplies: Lego plastic construction toys, magazines, paper bags

Preparation: Gather pictures of homes or buildings from magazines. You'll need one picture for each pair. Sort a variety of Lego pieces (at least twenty) into paper bags.

Have preteens form pairs. Have them sit down, back-to-back. Give one partner in each pair a bag of Legos and the other partner a picture. Partners shouldn't show either their pictures or Lego pieces to each other.

Say: **The object of this game is to build a Lego structure that closely resembles the picture your team was given, without the builder ever actually seeing the picture. When I say "go," the person who is holding the picture must try to describe how to re-create it to the person with the bag of Legos. Both of you need to communicate clearly without turning around and looking at your partner's item. You'll have three minutes. After three minutes, we'll all compare what we created.**

When three minutes are up, have teams show each other their buildings. Ask:

- **What was it like trying to describe the picture?**
- **How hard was it to build the object your partner described?**
- **How did you encourage each other during this game?**
- **You were forced to only use words in this game. What are some other ways you can encourage others?** ▪

TIRE BALANCE
tire balance

Topic Connections: Use this game to challenge kids to evaluate, brainstorm, and talk through problems as a team.

Game Overview: Preteens will help each other stay balanced on tires.

Energy Level: Medium

Supplies: Old tires (fifteen-inch work best)

Preparation: Collect enough tires for your group. (Tire stores have old tires awaiting recycling they could loan.)

Divide your preteens into groups of eight or nine. Give each group a tire.

Say: **Each group must work together to get all the people in your group on top of your tire at the same time. You can do whatever you want, but no one can touch the ground, walls, or any other support. Once there, I'll ask questions that each team member must answer. Let's see which team can stay balanced on the tire the longest.**

Wait until all the teams are balanced on the tires, then ask:

• **What is your favorite food?**

• **What is your favorite sport?**

• **What was the name of your first pet?**

• **What kind of music do you like best?**

• **Where is your favorite place to go on vacation?**

After the game is over, ask:

• **What was the hardest part about this game?**

• **How did you help each other stay balanced?**

• **What are some other ways you can help one another?**

HOW MUCH DO YOU KNOW?
how much do you know?

Topic Connections: Use this game to challenge kids' listening and memory skills.

Game Overview: Preteens will quickly think of items in various categories.

Energy Level: Medium

Supplies: None

Preparation: Prior to playing this game, come up with several categories that your kids will be familiar with. Topics should be broad enough that your preteens will be able to come up with several answers—for example, songs that contain the word "love," movies about space, or women from the Bible.

Have preteens form equal-sized numbered groups of up to ten, and have groups sit in circles.

Say: **I am going to give you a topic and you will have two minutes to brainstorm as many answers as possible. For example, if the topic is space movies, you could give answers like** *Star Wars, Star Trek,* **and** *2001: A Space Odyssey.* **But you must** *remember* **your group's answers, because you may not write anything down in this game.**

I will start with Group 1 and ask for its first answer, then Group 2, Group 3, and so on. If a group is unable to come up with an answer, or gives an answer already presented by another group, it will be out for the rest of this round. We will continue on this topic until only one group is still able to answer.

Play several rounds of the game. Then ask:

• **How did your team's listening skills help you in this game?**

• **How hard was it to remember what answers your team came up with?**

• **How can listening and remembering skills help you in your life?**

WILD & WACKY GAMES

he one thing you can count on when working with preteens is that they like to have fun. Wild fun. Wacky fun. Outrageous fun. Well, these games fit *that* bill! Some are messy, some are wet, some are disgusting—but they're all fun!

AQUA BONNET
aquabonnet

Topic Connections: This game is just for fun, but you might bring out how the best players are likely to get the most wet, and this is like how serving God may be uncomfortable.

Game Overview: Participants will try to catch water balloons on top of their heads in plastic baskets.

Energy Level: High

Supplies: Milk jugs, water balloons, scissors, cloth strips

Preparation: Collect enough empty gallon milk jugs for each player to have one. You will also need to gather long strips of cloth, at least 24 inches long and 2-3 inches wide. Cut off the top of each jug and cut two slits in the base. Insert a long strip of cloth through the slits. The ends of the strip will be tied under a player's chin. (See illustration.) Fill dozens of water balloons to launch during the game.

egin the game by asking players to tie the "bonnets" to their heads by securing the fabric strips in a knot under the chin. Divide the group into teams of five or six.

Say: **I will toss water balloons into the air and you should try to catch as many as you can in your aqua bonnet. Your team should designate a spot to pile its balloons as they are caught. Afterward, balloons will be counted and the team catching the most will win. Broken balloons will not be counted.**

Carefully pitch the balloons into the air, alternating between teams. ▚

SPITWAD DARTBOARD
s p i t w a d d a r t b o a r d

Topic Connections: This game is just for fun but it could preface a lesson on sin, since by definition, sin implies a missing of the mark or target.

Game Overview: Participants will shoot paper wads through straws at a point board.

Energy Level: Medium

Supplies: Straws, scrap paper, poster board, glue stick, masking tape, marker

Preparation: Cut a large circle out of blue poster board. Use the glue stick to affix it to white poster board. Cut a slightly smaller circle out of yellow poster board and glue it inside the blue circle. Complete the bull's-eye by cutting a smaller red circle and pasting it inside the yellow circle. Using a black marker, label the red circle "100," the yellow circle "50," and the blue circle "10."

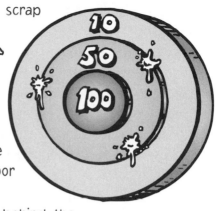

egin by distributing straws and scrap paper to all participants. By using paper of different colors, each player's spitwads would be easy to identify on the board. Attach the point board to a wall in your room or outside on the wall of a building. Create a line with masking tape on the floor about ten feet from the point board.

Ask preteens to form three lines behind the tape. The first person in each line should shoot three wads, keeping track of the total score. When they have finished, they can go to the end of their lines, and the next three participants should take a turn. Continue as long as desired. ■

PUFFY WIG RACE
puffy wig race

Topic Connections: This is a just-for-fun game that might be good to set the tone for a discussion of body-image.

Game Overview: Participants will race to attach marshmallows to the heads of their teammates at the other end of the room.

Energy Level: High

Supplies: Shower caps, jars of marshmallow creme, miniature marshmallows, masking tape

Preparation: Set up your playing area by placing a chair for every team at one end of the room and a masking-tape starting line at the other end.

onsider playing this game outdoors since the relay requires a lot of space and it could be messy. Divide your group into teams of ten or less. Each team should choose a volunteer to wear the shower-cap wig. When individuals have been chosen, ask them to take a seat in a chair at the far end of the playing field. Provide a shower cap for each volunteer to wear.

Next, distribute jars of marshmallow creme and ask players to cover their teammate's shower cap with it.

When they have finished, give each team a bag of miniature marshmallows, direct them to the starting line, and say: **When I say "go," all members of your team at once should take one marshmallow, race to the other end, place it on your teammate's puffy wig, and run back to the starting line where they will get another marshmallow. Repeat this process until all of your team's marshmallows have been carried one by one and placed upon your teammate's head.**

Consider taking pictures of the puffy wigs to hang in your meeting room. The portraits could be cropped into oval shapes and attached to centers of dollar bills for a creative board display. ◼

CONE HEAD RING TOSS
c o n e h e a d r i n g t o s s

Topic Connections: This is a fun game for varied occasions and settings.

Game Overview: Participants will try to ring hoops on their partners' heads.

Energy Level: Medium

Supplies: Stopwatch, newspaper, masking tape, plastic foam plates, sunglasses

Preparation: Cut the centers out of foam plates to create dozens of rings.

Ask preteens to find partners. Place two tape lines on the floor, four to five feet apart. Next, have each pair create a cone using newspaper and tape. Help kids twist the newspaper, taping the outside until the paper fits snugly like a cap. Then place the cone on top of one player's head (see diagram). Also give the cone-head player a pair of sunglasses to wear.

Give each pair five or six rings (each team should have an equal number of rings).

Direct participants to the lines on the floor and say: **Partners should stand behind these lines facing one another with the gap between them.**

Ask all teams to take their places and say: **When I say go, you will race to ring as many hoops as you can on your partner's head.**

Set your watch for the desired time and begin!

MAKE YOUR MARK
make your mark

Topic Connections: This fun game could also be used with a discussion about friendships.

Game Overview: Kids will "make their mark" on others' shirts in this wild-and-crazy game. By the end of the game, everyone will have an autographed shirt as a memento of class!

Energy Level: High

Supplies: Traffic cones, white T-shirts, colorful watercolor (nonpermanent) markers

Preparation: Mark off a large area with cones. You'll need at least a space of thirty feet by thirty feet.

Gather everyone in a circle and have each preteen put on his or her white T-shirt. It's a good idea to have kids wear the shirt over their regular clothes. Hand out markers and tell kids that they will "make their mark" on their classmates' shirts.

Say: **The object of the game is to mark your initials on as many of your classmates' shirts as possible. At the same time, try to keep your classmates from marking on your shirt. You can only mark on the back or arms of the shirt. Anyone who marks anywhere else is disqualified and must sit out of the game.**

Also take a minute to think about a simple symbol that represents who you are. You might think of a cross, a smiley face, a sun, or a music note. If you're able to mark someone with your initials as well as your special symbol, you get a million, katrillion bonus points! You've got one minute to make your mark on as many people as possible. Ready...go!

Allow kids a minute to mark their classmates' shirts. At the end of one minute, see who has the least amount of initials on his or her shirt. Then see who marked initials on the most shirts. Finally, take note of who was able to mark a symbol on someone else's shirt. After the game, take time to allow everyone to initial all the shirts, so that everyone has a memento of the game. ◪

MONKEY SANDWICHES

Topic Connections: This fun game could also be used to talk about cooperation or teamwork.

Game Overview: In this disgustingly crazy game, pairs race to be the first to completely eat a peanut butter and jelly sandwich prepared with their feet.

Energy Level: High

Supplies: Bread, peanut butter, jelly, food storage bags, rubber bands, tarp/large trash bags, soap, water, towels, tape

Preparation: Put a tarp or several large plastic trash bags on the floor and secure it with tape. Place several jars of peanut butter and several jars of jelly on the tarp or bags and secure them with tape. Spread the jars out so that there is about four to five feet between each set.

Have preteens form pairs and give each pair two slices of bread. Ask them to sit down on the tarp, fairly near to one set of peanut butter and jelly.

Say: **The object of this game is to make a peanut butter and jelly sandwich and eat it as fast as you can. However, this peanut butter and jelly sandwich is going to be prepared in a special way.**

Whoever has a birthday closest to today, please take off your shoes and socks—you will make this sandwich using only your feet. Place the food storage bags over your feet and secure the bags around your ankles using rubber bands. After your sandwich is prepared, feed it to your partner using only your feet.

After all students are done with the contest, have kids remove the bags from their feet and allow everyone to wash up. ■

GUMBALL MOUSE
gumball mouse

Topic Connections: Here's a game to play just for fun.

Game Overview: Students will compete in teams of five or six people to see who can complete a relay and sculpt a gum-ball statue first.

Energy Level: High

Supplies: Gum balls, plastic spoons, plastic trash bags, disposable gloves

Preparation: Place the gum balls in a large bowl in the center of the room. Spread out the trash bags on the floor around the edge of the room—all equidistant from the bowl of gum balls. Make sure that there is one trash-bag station for each group of students.

Divide up your students into groups of five or six people and send one group to each trash-bag station. Each group must choose one person to be its Gum-Ball Machine. Once groups have designated a Gum-Ball Machine, have that person kneel in the middle of the trash bag.

The other kids on each team will then line up next to their Gum-Ball Machine, facing the bowl of gum balls. Give each person a spoon.

Say: **There are two parts to this game. The first person in your line will hold the spoon in his or her mouth and when I say "go," will run to the bowl of gum balls, scoop one out with the spoon, run back to your Gum-Ball Machine, and drop it into his or her mouth. The next person in line then repeats the same process. The Gum-Ball Machine will begin to chew up the gum balls as soon as they are dropped into his or her mouth. If you drop a gum ball, you must go back and get a new one.**

Your team will continue to do this until you cannot fit any more gum balls into your Machine's mouth. At that point, the Gum-Ball Machine must spit out the wad of gum and the entire team must put on gloves and sculpt a mouse with the chewed gum. ■

CEREAL HEAD
c e r e a l h e a d

Topic Connections: This is another messy and fun game for your preteens.

....

Game Overview: Kids will compete in teams of five or six to see which group can get the most cereal to stick to their team member's shaving cream-covered face.

Energy Level: Medium

Supplies: Tarp or large plastic bags, tape, cereal, canned whipped cream, plastic spoons, sunglasses, watch

Preparation: Put a tarp (or several large plastic trash bags) on the floor, and secure it with tape. If you have the option, this is a great game to play outdoors.

ivide preteens into groups of five or six and ask each group to choose one person to be the Cereal Catcher. Have the Cereal Catchers kneel in a line on the tarp or trash bags. Have them close their eyes and mouths and pinch noses. Carefully spray a layer of whipped cream on their faces. It needs to cover a large enough area of their faces, and be thick enough, so that there is ample room for the cereal to stick. Have the Cereal Catchers each put on a pair of sunglasses.

Next, have the other kids on each team form a line, three to four feet across from their teammates. Give the first person in each line a plastic spoon and a bowl of cereal.

Say: **When I say "go," you will have ten seconds to use your plastic spoon and shoot as much cereal as possible onto your teammate's face. After ten seconds I'll yell "switch," and the next person in line will have ten seconds to accomplish the same thing. This will continue until everyone in your line has had a turn.**

BOX HEAD CROSSING
box head crossing

Topic Connections: This fun game could also be used in discussing communication or overcoming obstacles.

Game Overview: This is a simple relay game in which preteens must run from one corner of the room to another with boxes on their heads—while crossing through the path of the other competing teams.

Energy Level: High

Supplies: Cardboard boxes

Preparation: None

Divide preteens into teams of eight. (If you have more than thirty-five kids in your group, you'll want to have at least two relay circles.) Each team will then split into two groups of four and will form two lines—facing each other and across the room from each other. Give a cardboard box to the first person in each line on one side of the room. For example, if you have three teams of eight competing against each other, there will be six lines of four kids in a circle around the room (see diagram).

The first student in Group A of Teams 1, 2, and 3 will receive a box.

Say: **When I say "go," put the box on your head and run across the circle to your teammates on the other side. Once you get there, the first person in that line must take the box, put it on his or her head, and run to the other side of the circle. The object of this game is to get all eight people to the opposite side of the circle first.** ◼

BIG FOOT
big foot

Topic Connections: This is a fun game that could also be used when discussing guarding your heart or hurting others.

Game Overview: Preteens will try to pop balloons tied to others' ankles while protecting their own balloons.

Energy Level: High

Supplies: Balloons, yarn or string

Preparation: For every game round, blow up enough balloons for each player to have one (plus a few extra). Cut two-foot lengths of string or yarn. Mark off a boundary using chairs or tables. You want to have a large enough area for kids to move freely, but not so large that kids can simply run away from each other.

Have preteens remove their shoes (they can leave their socks on if they wish). Provide each player a balloon and yarn to tie it to his or her ankle. The balloon should be about one foot away from the ankle when tied. Say: **The object of this game is to stomp on the other players' balloons and pop them. But at the same time, you have to keep your balloon from being popped by another player. When your balloon is popped, you're out for this round. As fewer players are left, I'll make the boundaries of the game smaller.**

TIP — **For an even greater challenge,** use two balloons instead of one. You could either tie one balloon to each ankle, or tie both to one ankle.

When you see kids can move more than about six feet from one another, begin moving the boundaries in several feet on all sides. Play the game a few rounds. ◼

BALLOON BOOMERANG
balloon boomerang

Topic Connections: This fun game could also be used with a discussion of how our words can't be taken back.

Game Overview: Preteens will try to toss water balloons into buckets guarded by other players.

Energy Level: High

Supplies: Water balloons, large buckets or ice coolers

Preparation: Fill lots of water balloons.

Have the group form teams of up to ten. Have teams line up about twenty feet away from a bucket or ice cooler. Each team will need its own bucket or cooler. Then have each team choose a Boomeranger. The Boomeranger will guard the bucket, so have him or her go stand next to the bucket when chosen. Say: **When you throw a boomerang correctly, it should come back to you. Well in this game, our boomerangs are water balloons, and they** work just the opposite of a boomerang. The object of our game is to toss the water balloons in the bucket. If you miss, the Boomeranger will pick it up if it doesn't break (or catch it if it's going to miss the bucket), and toss it back to you. If the balloon does go into the bucket, you become the new Boomeranger.

You may want to either shorten or lengthen the distance between the kids and the buckets, if the game is either too easy or too difficult.

Play until all the water balloons are gone. ◼

GAMES FOR SPECIAL DAYS

Holidays are great times to have fun with preteens. These games will make a connection to various holidays. Some games are just for fun, others can be used to teach on a topic, and a few are designed for special days and events apart from holidays. Make your time special with your preteens using these special days games!

NEW YEAR'S RESOLUTIONS
new year's day

Topic Connections: Use this game to teach preteens about overcoming obstacles.

Game Overview: Preteens will write New Year's resolutions and navigate through an obstacle course.

Energy Level: Low

Supplies: Index cards, pens, blindfolds, chairs or other obstacles, tape

Preparation: None

You'll need an indoor open area to play this game. Provide index cards and pens to preteens. Say: **I want you to think of three New Year's resolutions you would like to make and list them on your card. You're then going to navigate blindfolded through an obstacle course, trying to reach the "goal" wall over here** [indicate wall].

After kids have written on their cards, have them form pairs and provide one blindfold to each pair. Have pairs choose who will wear the blindfold first. While kids put on blindfolds, place chairs or other obstacles in a random pattern, between the kids and the goal wall. Say: **In your pairs, you have a blindfolded player and a Pilot. Pilots, your job is to yell out directions, so your blindfolded partner doesn't run into any chairs or other obstacles. You can't touch your partner at any time. Blindfolded players, you're trying to get to the goal wall so you can tape your resolutions there. If you hit a chair, you must sit down in the chair and count to ten before proceeding. Pilots, spin your partner around one time.**

Begin the game. Have tape available at the wall for preteens to tape their list of resolutions. After everyone has made it to the wall, have pairs change roles and run the obstacle course a second time. Ask:

• **What was it like trying to navigate the obstacle course this way?**

• **When you bumped into an obstacle, you had to sit and wait. How is this like or unlike when you face obstacles in life?**

• **What obstacles could you face with the resolutions you wrote on your cards?**

• **How can God help you overcome those obstacles?** ▪

GOD'S HEART FOR YOU
v a l e n t i n e ' s d a y

Topic Connections: Use this game to affirm preteens with God's love.

Game Overview: Preteens will write ways God loves them on heart handouts.

Energy Level: Medium

Supplies: "God's Love Is for You!" handout (p. 89), pens, watch or timer, valentine hearts candy

Preparation: Photocopy one "God's Love Is for You!" handout (p. 89) for each player.

ive each preteen a copy of the "God's Love Is for You!" handout and a pen. Show kids a candy heart and say: **These candy hearts have** little sayings on them to show appreciation or love. As fun as it is to receive these words, we have a greater way to receive love. I want you to each go up to as many people as possible and write one way God loves this person on his or her heart paper. For example, you could write, "God created you in a special way."

While you're writing on someone's heart, that person should also write on yours. Let's see how many people we can share God's love with!

Set a time limit based on how many kids you have. Allow two minutes for every ten kids. Pass out the candies to everyone. Ask:

- **How does it feel to have these words written on your hearts?**
- **How is God's love for you the ultimate valentine?** ◪

RESURRECTION RELAY

e a s t e r

Topic Connections: Use this game to teach preteens about sharing the good news of Jesus.

Game Overview: Preteens will experience the excitement of the empty tomb in this relay game.

Energy Level: High

Supplies: Long folding tables

Preparation: Set up tables end-to-end along one side of a wall (you'll need one table for every two relay teams).

Have preteens form relay teams of up to eight kids. Have teams line up about twenty feet from the line of tables. Kids will heel-and-toe walk to the empty tomb (the table) and touch the top of it. Then players will crawl under the table and say, "Anybody in here?" before crawling out, running back, and tagging the next person by saying, "The tomb is empty! Jesus is alive!" When the relay is complete, ask:

- **What emotions did you feel playing this game?**
- **What emotions do you think the disciples felt when they discovered Jesus was alive?**
- **Why is it exciting to know Jesus was raised from the dead?**
- **How can you be excited when telling others about Jesus?** ◪

God's Love Is for You!

- -

God's Love Is for You!

- -

MOM'S TYPICAL DAY
mother's day

Topic Connections: Use this game to teach preteens about appreciating others.

. . . .

Game Overview: Preteens will experience a hard day in the life of a mother.

Energy Level: Medium

Supplies: Mouse pad, paper plate, sock or T-shirt, stuffed animal

Preparation: None

You'll need one adult or teen volunteer (preferably a female) to play the mother role for this game. Form four equal relay teams (Team A, Team B, and so on), and direct each team to a different corner of a room. Have your volunteer "mother" stand in the middle of the room. Give one team the mouse pad, one team a paper plate, another team a sock or T-shirt, and the last team a stuffed animal. Say: **Each of these objects represents some of the things your moms do on a daily basis— things like cooking, cleaning, taking care of pets, and going to work. That's a lot to do! When I say, "Happy Mother's Day!" the first person on each team will toss his or her object to our "mother" and run to the back of the line. Our mother will catch or pick up these objects and toss them randomly to the four teams. For example, if she catches a plate from Team A she could toss it to Team D. She will be busily trying to catch and throw the objects at all times. The next person on each team will then throw his or her object to our mother, and repeat until everyone has thrown and caught an object.**

Say: **Happy Mother's Day!** to begin the game. After everyone has thrown and caught an object, the game is over. Ask the volunteer mother:

• **What was it like trying to catch and throw all these objects?**

• **How is this like a mother trying to handle a busy day?**

Ask preteens:

• **How does this game give you more appreciation of what our mothers do for us?**

• **What's one way you show your thanks to your mother?** ◨

SCHOOL'S OUT
s c h o o l v a c a t i o n

Topic Connections: This is a fun end-of-school game that could be used to discuss having healthy fun or recreation.

Game Overview: Preteens will celebrate a break from school by acting out summer activities.

Energy Level: High

Supplies: Paper bags, bubble gum, squirt guns, cereal, paper cups, scrap paper, small trash can, chairs, "Summertime Fun" handout

Preparation: Make enough copies of the "Summertime Fun!" handout (p. 92) for each team to have a set. Cut apart the strips, and tape bubble gum to appropriate handout strips. Place one set of eight strips (from the handout) in each bag. Put a small amount of cereal in a paper cup for each team. Set up two chairs—the "car" chair and the "roller coaster" chair. Also place a trash can about ten feet away from a pile of scrap paper.

You'll need to set up the various activities and supplies (listed on the handout strips) in various areas in your room. Form relay teams of up to eight preteens per team. Place the prepared paper bag about ten to fifteen feet in front of each team. Say: **School's out! Summertime is here! Let's celebrate all the fun things we can do this summer! The first player in each team will run up to this bag, and without looking inside the bag, reach in and pull out one strip of paper. On those paper strips are instructions for you.**

Before you begin show kids the locations of the "car," "roller coaster," "basketball court," cups of cereal, and squirt guns. To begin the game, say: **School's out!** You might want to have some snacks afterward and talk about what kids have planned for their summers. ◨

SUMMERTIME FUN!

1. Chew this gum and blow a big bubble!

2. Run and grab a squirt gun. Guess what you get to do with it? (Squirt each person on your team and then put it back where you found it, please.)

3. Find the "car chair," sit down in the car, and say, "Are we there yet?" three times.

4. Find the "roller coaster chair," sit down on it, throw your arms up in the air, and scream!

5. You're on the summer swim team. "Swim" back and forth three laps (imitating the crawl stroke).

6. Now you have time to eat breakfast. Scarf down a cup of cereal.

7. Basketball camp! Crumple up some paper and shoot three shots at the trash can.

8. You landed a summer job! Go up to each team member and ask, "Do you want fries with that?"

DAD'S REVENGE SCAVENGER HUNT
father's day

Topic Connections: This is a just-for-fun game that could be used before discussing appearance or searching after things of the world.

Game Overview: Preteens will search for ugly ties.

Energy Level: Medium

Supplies: Old ugly ties

Preparation: Hide the ties in your playing area.

Here's a way to get rid of all your preteens' dads' ugly ties. Contact kids' dads and ask for ugly tie donations. Then hide them either inside or outside and have a scavenger hunt. Once all the ties have been found, have kids try to guess whose dad the ties belonged to. Then tie the ties together making a long rope and have a tug-of-war contest! ◼

FIRE BRIGADE
independence day

Topic Connections: This fun water game could be used to discuss the importance of teamwork.

Game Overview: Preteens will pass water down a line using cups held by their teeth.

Energy Level: Medium

Supplies: Buckets, paper cups

Preparation: Fill one water bucket for each relay team.

Say: **It sure is hot in July! Let's cool off!**

Have kids form equal-number teams of up to ten and line up. For each team, place a water-filled bucket at one end of the line and an empty bucket at the other end of the line (see diagram on page 94). Give each player a small paper cup.

When you say "go!" have the first member in line place the cup in his or her teeth and dip the cup in the water. He or she will then pour the water into the cup held by the teeth of the next player in line. Continue going down the line to the last player, who will dump his or her cup of water into the empty bucket. You may set a time limit or let the game continue until the water is gone. ◼

THOUGHT FOR THE DAY
b a c k t o s c h o o l

Topic Connections: This is an affirmation game that could be used to discuss encouragement.

Game Overview: Kids will guess who wrote a saying in their school day planners. This game works especially well with small, close-knit groups.

Energy Level: Low

Supplies: Pens or pencils; Bibles, concordances, or books of quotations (optional); one student pocket calendar or student day planner (such as the *Student Plan-It*, junior high edition, Group Publishing) per student.

Preparation: Each preteen will need a pen or pencil and a pocket calendar or day planner. Make sure the calendar reflects the school calendar year. If you choose to use reference books, spread them out in a long line in the middle of the room.

Have the group form pairs and sit on the floor back to back. If you're using reference books, have everyone sit in a close circle around the reference books. Hand each person a pocket calendar and a pen or pencil, and tell kids to mark their names in the books so that they know which one is theirs. Say: **School is starting soon, and this calendar will help to keep you on top of when your homework is due or when you might have practice. But with this game, your calendar will also help you remember other things that are important in your daily schedule.**

Take fifteen seconds to shuffle the calendars. In that fifteen seconds, at random call out "left," "right," or "over." When you say "left," have kids keep passing the calendars to the left. When you say "right," have kids keep passing the calendars to the right. When you say "over," have kids pass the calendars over their heads to the next person.

When the calendars are shuffled, give everyone up to a minute to find a date in the calendar they're holding that's important to them and write a quote on that date. They might choose birthdays, their favorite holidays, or dates that marked particular milestones in their spiritual journeys.

Tell them to write a favorite Scripture or quote in the dates they chose. The sayings don't have to be famous, they can be something they remember their parents saying, or something they heard in a sermon. They can also be simple sayings, such as "Be happy," or "God loves you." Give kids a minute to write something in that calendar.

If you have time, shuffle the calendars again, and have students write a second quote in the calendars. You might even repeat the activity a third or fourth time.

Once kids have finished, have each student take a turn to flip through his or her calendar, read one of the sayings, and try to guess who wrote the saying and why that date might be important to that person.

Close in a prayer, asking God to guide students in times of pressure and stress throughout the school year, and that they will remember what's truly important in their lives. ◧

STUFF THE (LIVE) TURKEY
thanksgiving

Topic Connections: This is a fun holiday game.

Game Overview: Preteens will toss paper "stuffing" into a trash can "turkey."

Energy Level: Medium

Supplies: Scrap paper, newsprint, trash can, tape

Preparation: Roll up two sheets of newsprint and tape the rolls, making baton "wings."

Place a trash can in the center of the room. Ask for one preteen volunteer to be the "turkey wings." Give him or her the two rolled-up paper tubes. Have the turkey lie down on his or her back next to the trash can, and practice swinging the paper tube wings around the opening of the trash can. The other students can sit around the turkey, not closer than ten feet away. Give them plenty of wadded paper. Say: **When you cook a turkey, you put stuffing inside it. Well, this is our turkey. The trash can is the part you stuff, and** [volunteer's name] **is this turkey's wings. Normally, you stuff a dead turkey, but our turkey is very much alive, so it does** *not* **want to be stuffed! So while you try to "stuff" our turkey by tossing wadded paper stuffing into the trash can, the turkey's wings will attempt to bat away your paper stuffing.**

Say: **Gobble, gobble!** to start the game. Play a round for a few minutes, and then take turns alternating new volunteers to be the turkey's wings with each new round of play. ◼

TREE-TRIMMING RELAY
christmas

Topic Connections: Use this game during the Christmas season.

Game Overview: In this relay race to decorate Christmas trees, kids will have your room decorated for the season in no time!

Energy Level: High

Supplies: Christmas tree decorating supplies, one tabletop-sized Christmas tree for every five or six preteens

Preparation: For every Christmas tree you use, you'll need the same number of decorations, such as tree lights, tinsel, candy canes, ornaments, and stars or angels for the top of the trees. If you need decorating hooks or yarn to hang ornaments on the trees, prepare the ornaments prior to the relay. You may also want to have kids make their own ornaments out of construction paper, poster board, or other craft supplies prior to the relay.

Place the Christmas trees and their accessories at one end of the room. Have preteens line up at the other end in groups of five or six. Tell your group that this relay race is going to be a speedy way to "deck the halls." When you say "go," the first person on each team must run to a Christmas tree, select one decoration or set of decorations, and place them on the tree. Then those players must run back to their teams, tag-up, and let the next kids in line race to the trees and decorate.

If you have enough time, or when it's time to take down Christmas decorations, you might have a tree-*untrimming* relay! ◼

FOOTBALL FRENZY
f o o t b a l l f r e n z y

Topic Connections: This is a fun game that can be used during kickoff weekend or sometime during the football season.

Game Overview: Preteens will pass a football down a line using their feet. The last person in line will "kick" the ball toward "goal posts."

Energy Level: Medium

Supplies: Football

Preparation: none

Have preteens remove their shoes and lie down on their backs in a line of about eight. Use additional footballs and lines for larger groups. Give a football to the player at one end of the line. He or she must balance the football and pass it down the line to the next person. Players keep passing the ball until it gets to the last person. When the ball is there, have the first two kids in the line get up and become goal posts. They do this by standing

TIP

There are a few fun variations of this game. One is to use two footballs and have kids pass the ball down the line starting from both ends. Another idea is to make one long line with larger groups. See if kids can negotiate a successful passing down the longer line. Another variation is to have preteens pass the football with feet around a circle while listening to sports music. When the music stops, the person with the ball kicks it through the goal posts.

about ten feet away from the player with the ball and spacing themselves about six to ten feet apart (see illustration). Then have the last player attempt to "kick" the ball through the goal posts. Continue playing additional rounds by having players each shift one space after each successful football passing and kicking. ◼

HUMAN BIRTHDAY PRESENTS
human birthday presents

Topic Connections: This is a fun game to celebrate upcoming (or current) birthdays.

Game Overview: Preteens will race to wrap birthday celebrants in wrapping paper.

Energy Level: Medium

Supplies: Wrapping paper, bows, tape, watch or timer

Preparation: None

Form relay teams of four or five kids per team. Have the person in each group whose birthday is closest to today's date become the "present." Say: **To celebrate these kids' upcoming birthdays, let's give them a present. When I say, "Happy Birthday!" your team is to quickly decorate from shoulders down, your human present. You'll have one minute.**

Say: **Happy Birthday!** to begin the game. After one minute, stop the decorating and have kids vote on the best-decorated person. You might want to serve birthday cake and drinks after this game. ◼

section **nine**
On-THE-ROAD GAMES

ou pile the preteen group into the church van and head off to Waterland. To avoid the chorus of, "Are we there *yet*?" try these fun games designed to be played during road trips.

You'll find a variety of fun and exciting games to pass the time whether you're traveling through towns with street lights, or traveling for hours along the long and boring freeways. There are games sure to challenge your kids with words, numbers, rhymes, musical rhythms, art, and just plain quick-witted silliness.

Because these games all share some things in common with each other, some details are included here. Enjoy your trip!

Ways to Time Games: Timing games adds a mental challenge to the play and keeps kids' anticipation high. Here are some creative ways of timing games if you don't have a stopwatch or the availability of a second hand on a watch.

• Have the driver use the odometer (or trip odometer) and designate the number of miles that each play of the game will last. The driver will call out when the game begins and ends.

• Designate a person to count aloud slowly, "one thousand one, one thousand two, one thousand-three..." to a number you designate, then yell "stop."

• If you're in the city, have your designated Timer (one of the kids) count light posts. For example, if you decide the game should last for twenty light posts, have your designated person count the light posts aloud until the car or van reaches the twentieth light post.

• If you're on the freeway, have your designated Timer count the small mileage posts on the side of the road. For example, if you decide the game should last for five miles, have your designated person count the mileage posts out loud until the car or van reaches the fifth post. Mileage signs will work also, but they aren't positioned at even distances.

BACK-WORDS BETSY (OR BEN)

Best Played: On roads with signs and billboards

Energy Level: Moderately paced

Supplies: None

Length of Play: Each round takes about three minutes. A van of seven people playing takes about twenty minutes.

Start by choosing a person to be the designated Timer. Choose another person to be "Back-Words Betsy (or Ben)" and have the Timer give him or her thirty seconds to look at the signs and billboards to find a word he or she can say backward. Encourage the players to choose large words that will be harder for others to guess.

When the Back-Words Betsy (or Ben) has found a word, the round of play begins when he or she says the word backward loud enough for everyone to hear. Encourage the players to quickly take turns guessing what word was said backward.

A clipboard and pen are helpful for your visual learners. The person whose turn it is can write down his or her word backward in large letters for everyone to see as well as say the backward word. If the players accidentally write letters backward, it's OK. It will just give an added challenge to the game.

If the person guesses correctly, he or she becomes the next Back-Words Betsy (or Ben) and chooses a new word to say backward. If the players take more than thirty seconds to guess the word they think was said backward, the play proceeds to the next player.

Continue the game until everyone has had a chance to be Back-Words Betsy (or Ben).

"I'D RATHER"
"i'd rather"

Best Played: Anywhere

Energy Level: Moderately paced

Supplies: None

Length of Play: About two minutes. End the game after about twenty minutes, before the players begin to get bored with it. You'll want players to look forward to playing it again later.

Before beginning "I'd Rather," choose the preteen who has the most "stuff" piled around him or her, and let him or her decide which way the turns will go. For example, he or she may choose to start with the person that is farthest from the driver and have the turns proceed clockwise from there.

Say: **The purpose of this game is to quickly think of places or things** you'd rather be doing than sitting in this van. As everyone adds a new vacation spot, we'll be building our dream itinerary—a list of places we'd all like to go on vacation.

The game will start with [name of person who will start the game] saying [his or her] **favorite place to go. For example,** [he or she] **could say, "Driving to camp is nice, but on my vacation, I'd rather be on the South Sea Islands."**

Tell the players they could choose someplace like Disneyland or bungee jumping off the arm of the Statue of Liberty—they can use real places or make up their own wild activities.

If many of your teens struggle with lists, simplify the game by suggesting they only give names of places and not activities until they're more comfortable with the game.

Say: **The next person will say the place that** [name of the starting person] **said, then add his or her own vacation spot or activity. And the game will continue until someone forgets to say the itinerary in the right order or takes more than thirty seconds to think of a place or activity that hasn't been said before.** (Example: "Going to Disneyland, walking across the Golden Gate Bridge, playing laser tag, riding a horse, and bike racing is fun, but I'd rather be riding the white-water rapids.")

As each round of play ends, play again. Encourage players to keep the game moving quickly for more excitement and fun. ∎

ALPHABET POPPERS
alphabet poppers

Best Played: Expressways, country roads, or long city streets

Energy Level: Fast-paced

Supplies: none

Length of Play: Twenty to thirty minutes. End the game when the players are still enjoying it, so they will want to play again a few hours down the road.

Choose the person that was born the farthest away from where you are now to start the game. Play should move clockwise.

Say: **This game is played in alphabetical order, but the tricky part is that the game starts and stops at either red lights or stop signs.**

When the car comes to a complete stop, the person who starts will say the first word that "pops" into his or her head that begins with the letter A. The next person will say the first word that pops into his or her head that begins with the letter B, the next person C, until we finish with the letter Z, or until the car comes to a stop at a stop sign or red light.

Here's the challenge: The game has to move fast so we can complete the entire alphabet before we come to the next stop sign or red light. If you take more than fifteen seconds to pop the next word, you'll be out of the game until the next round.

Have one round of practice from A to Z, then begin the game as soon as the car comes to a temporary stop. ◧

If you're on a long stretch of freeway with little or no traffic, tell players that the driver will start and stop the game by lightly pumping the brakes a few times at random intervals.

ROAD RACE
roadrace

Best Played: In the city or on roads where the speed limit changes often

Energy Level: Moderate to fast-paced

Supplies: Calculators or paper and pens (all optional)

Length of Play: It usually takes about three to five minutes for each round of play to reach 200 MPH. The total MPH can be adjusted according to the mathematical challenge your kids desire.

Designate a Police Officer to add the MPH sign numbers and "patrol" players that might miscalculate far ahead of where the actual total should be. The Police Officer should be someone who can accurately add numbers quickly in his or her head if you don't have a calculator.

Say: **For this game, we'll be "pushin' the limits" of the speed limit** on the road signs by adding up the numbers until they reach 200 MPH. But beware not to go over the speed limit and add more to your total than you should. If the Police Officer catches you, you'll have to subtract one hundred points from your total MPH.

Give the players paper and pens, or tell them they will be adding the MPH in their heads.

Say: **Tell the person next to you the type of car you'll be driving. When you're waiting for the next road sign to say the speed limit, shout out the speed you're going, then make the sound your revved engine would** make at that speed. You also can look behind you and count the speed limit signs on the opposite side of the road. When your car reaches 200 MPH, shout out, "Two hundred!" We'll wait until everyone reaches 200 MPH before we start the next race.

Fifth- and sixth-graders can add two-digit columns usually with no problem—the challenge is adding these two-digit numbers in their heads. Remind the players to be patient with themselves and with each other. Tell players that it's OK if they miss a number—they just continue adding the next number until they reach the 200 MPH goal.

Ready to start your engines? At the next speed limit sign, begin shouting out the speed your car is going and revving those engines.

When everyone has reached 200 MPH, begin new rounds of play. When you notice kids becoming disinterested, end the game before boredom begins to set in and the game no longer has the excitement factor.

Here are two variations: 1) Have players take turns being the Counter. The rest of the travelers will be the Shouters and shout out the numbers on the speed limit road signs as the car reaches the sign. The Counter must add the numbers either in his or her head or with a paper and pencil. When the Counter's total reaches 200 MPH, the game is over, and the next person begins a new game; or

2) Follow the same rules as the above variation 1, except have each row of seats be a designated team. Give each team of children a calculator to share as they increase their MPH up to 1,000 then back down to zero MPH. Your players who are less "math smart" will enjoy this variation the best. They can take turns using a calculator or they can be Shouters for their team. ■

RONALD RIGBY RHYMES
r o n a l d r i g b y r h y m e s

Best Played: Anywhere

Energy Level: Moderately paced

Supplies: none

Length of Play: Each round takes about three minutes. Play as long as kids are interested, about thirty minutes, before changing to another game to keep the interest high for next time's play.

Say: **To play each round of this game, we'll need to choose three people: a Rigby, a Storyteller, and the Judge.**

Starting from the front of the car, let players take turns being the Judge. The Judge will choose a Rigby to begin each round of the game. Then have Rigby choose a Storyteller from the rest of the players.

Say: **When it's your turn to be Rigby, it will be your job to think of four rhyming words to give to the Storyteller, such as kite, might, bite, night. The Storyteller will then tell**

Choose a Rigby by asking the players to make up a word with the funniest definition. Have the Judge designate the person with the most laughs to be Rigby.

us a story using those four words. **The story doesn't have to be long—maybe two or three sentences—something like, "One day when I was walking home in the dark a kite flew down behind me and said, 'Beware! I might bite you in the night.' So I turned around and said, 'Night kite, you might bite, but I can fight with all my might.' "**

But before we start, we have to introduce the game by chanting the introduction. Let's practice before we start. Have everyone chant the following rhyme about two or three times then continue.

There once was a man named Rigby, who had only four words to say.

(Hold up four fingers.)

He'd twitch and he'd itch,

(Twitch body, then scratch all over.)

Fall down in the ditch;

(Pretend to fall over.)

Then give the four words for the day.

Say: **Does everyone understand how to play? Let's begin.** Have players chant. Then have Rigby give the Storyteller the four rhyming words, and the game begins.

At the end of the story, have everyone cheer, then repeat the process of the game again. Continue playing for about thirty minutes, thirty miles, or until players seem to be repeating the same rhyming words.

FAST-FOOD FRENZY
fast-food frenzy

Best Played: After your break at a fast-food restaurant

Energy Level: Fast-paced

Supplies: Empty fast-food bag, scratch paper, and pen

Length of Play: About three to five song rounds

Preparation: Choose five to ten food items from the menu, such as French fries or nachos, and write the names on individual pieces of paper, fold the papers in half, and place them in the empty bag.

Choose the person who threw the most garbage away before leaving the restaurant to begin the game.

Say: **We're going to create some commercial jingles for fast-food restaurants like the one where we just stopped.** Hold up the bag. **In this bag I have subject titles such as** [name two items you have inside] **for the songs we'll create.** [Starting person's name] **will start our game by choosing** the subject from inside the bag then giving us an easy song tune such as "Old MacDonald Had a Farm" or "Jesus Loves Me." Have the Starter choose a title from the bag and announce the subject to the rest of the players. Give the Starter about thirty seconds to decide what song tune the players will be using.

For a fun variation, choose the number of words each of the players can sing when it's his or her turn.

Say: **The person sitting on** [the Starter's name]**'s right will begin our commercial jingle by making up** [his or her] **own words to the tune.** [He or she] **can make up as many words as** [he or she] **wants to add, then the person to the right continues the commercial jingle in the same way until the song is finished.** Begin playing.

When the jingle is finished, choose the next person and begin the game again. Continue making up jingles as long as kids desire to play.

CASA DE PICASSO
house of picasso

Best Played: Daytime

Energy Level: Fast-paced

Supplies: Clipboard, black paper, gel pens

Length of Play: Thirty seconds per player. Give each round of play about three to five miles. Most kids will still enjoy making new pictures up to about the fourth round. Switch to another game when kids begin to show disinterest, then bring the game back at a later time.

Preparation: Remembering to bring the supplies

Choose the person who guesses the closest interpretation of this game's title to be the Starter. Pass the colored pens around, and give the Starter the clipboard and paper.

Say: **Picasso was a famous painter and sculptor who lived from 1881-1973. He was famous for creating abstract art. None of his works of art looks realistic, and many people still have a hard time understanding what he was trying to say through his art—just like some people may** not understand the meaning of our game title.

We're going to create our own "Picasso." To make sure our Picasso doesn't look realistic, all of us are going to take turns adding on to our picture of a dream house. Ask:

• **How would you describe your perfect dream house?**

Let everyone answer.

Say: **Now that you've brain-stormed your ideas, let's begin creating our abstract work of art. First let's choose someone to be our Timer.**

If you have kids who don't want to participate in the drawing, suggest that they take turns being the Timer.

Choose the person sitting in the front passenger seat to be the Timer. Give the Timer a stopwatch or watch with a second hand, and have him or her give each player thirty seconds to add to the Casa De Picasso.

Say: **The Timer will give you thirty seconds to add a design to our Casa Del Picasso. When the thirty seconds is up, whether your drawing is finished or not, you must pass the clipboard to the next artist. Are you ready? Timer, start the seconds; Starter, begin our Casa De Picasso.** At the end of each thirty seconds, instruct the player to pass the clipboard to his or her right.

When the Casa De Picasso is complete, pass it to the Timer so he or she can hold it up for all to see.

To heighten the game's excitement and add more of a challenge, shorten the length of the players' turns to fifteen seconds. Make the maximum time for the completion of the Casa De Picasso three minutes, and tell kids that the goal is to fill in the entire page with color, leaving a half-inch border around the edge of the paper.

The Starter for the next round of play should be the player to the right of the artist who ended the previous Casa De Picasso. ∎

WHAT IF?

Best Played: Any time

....

Energy Level: Fast-paced

Supplies: None

Length of Play: Fifteen to twenty minutes. Give each of the players a maximum of thirty seconds; then have the next player continue the game.

This is a quick-witted, fast-paced game that stretches kids' creativity. Choose the person who last said, "Are we there yet?" to be the Starter for the game. Choose a Timer to monitor the players who might take more than thirty seconds for their turns. You might choose the person sitting closest to the driver or who is wearing the most articles of clothing. Give the Timer the

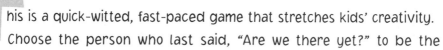

> **Encourage kids to make up wild and crazy** scenarios and answer back with the first thing that pops into their heads—the sillier the better.

stopwatch or watch with a second hand, and tell him or her to give each of the players thirty seconds for his or her turn.

Say: **The challenge to this game will be to quickly come up with wild and wacky questions like, "What if clouds rained down peanut butter and grape juice?" or "What if dogs barked with a yodel?"**

[Starter's name] **will start our game by saying "What if" then making up** [his or her] **own scenario.** [Name the person sitting on the Starter's right] **will**

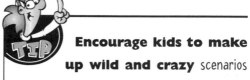

> **Give the players subjects** to create their scenarios from, such as animals, cities, colors, cars, teeth, food, science fiction, sports, or fashion.

answer the question with another silly answer like, "If dogs barked with a yodel, we'd all be singin' the blues."
Does everyone understand how to play? Practice one or two scenarios then begin the game. Play as long as kids show interest, then switch to another game. ◼

TOPIC CONNECTIONS INDEX
topic connections index

For more **amazing resources**

visit us at
group.com...

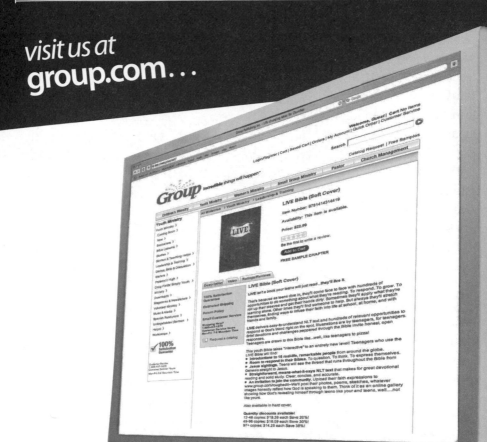

...or call us at
1-800-447-1070!